TURN YOUR *imagination* INTO MONEY

Ron Klein
Ray Giles

Morgan James Publishing • NEW YORK

TURN YOUR imagination INTO MONEY

Ron Klein / Ray Giles

ISBN: 1-933596-40-6 (Hardcover)
ISBN: 1-933596-58-9 (Paperback)
ISBN: 1-60037-034-9 (Audio)

Published by:

MORGAN · JAMES
THE ENTREPRENEURIAL PUBLISHER™
www.morganjamespublishing.com

Cover/Interior Design by:

Rachel Campbell
rcampbell77@cox.net

Morgan James Publishing, LLC
1225 Franklin Ave Ste 32
Garden City, NY 11530-1693
Toll Free 800-485-4943
www.MorganJamesPublishing.com

Habitat
for Humanity®
Peninsula
Building Partner

WANT to take your business (and your income) to the next level? Hard work alone won't do it for you; neither will merely improving your business or sales skills. More formal education by itself isn't the magic bullet, either. Those things count, but the one thing that separates the real winners from everyone else in the world can be summed up in two words: creative imagination.

"I've never before seen a book that lays out so clearly how to develop this special skill as 'Turn Your Imagination into Money' does. I wish I had known about it years ago. If you'd like to use your imagination to make your life infinitely better -- and I mean that quite literally -- then get 'Turn Your Imagination Into Money,' absorb its message, and start to live by its guidelines. The single most valuable skill I have is using my imagination to generate worthwhile ideas. It's been responsible for more success in my own life than anything else. If you'd like to get an unfair advantage that gives you an unbelievably powerful edge - get this book!"

DAVID GARFINKEL
Author
Advertising Headlines That Make You Rich

"Eureka!! That's exactly what you'll be shouting as you read this long lost gem unearthed by Ron Klein. To me, ideas are the lifeblood of my business. …With this little known resource you'll have all the ammo you need to put your brain into overdrive!"

YANIK SILVER
Author
33 Days to Online Profits
http://www.33daystoonlineprofits.com

"The truths in Turn Your Imagination Into Money are 100% as fresh and valid today as they were in 1933. I think the reader will find the 22 ways to spur imagination both helpful and practical. The nice thing is, the learning curve is simply the time it takes to read the simple discourse. But if applied, the results can be huge.

"There is so little imagination in much of business today. Particularly in the online marketing field, 90% of the people just do what they see the 10% of the leaders doing. This book shows how the 10% do what they do.

"It's simple. Practical. To-the-point. And an enlightening, joyful read."

MARLON SANDERS
CEO
Higher Response Marketing, Inc.
amazingformula.com

"Ray Giles timeless classic is as useful today as it was when written because the awesome power of creativity and imagination never change. Giles shows us how in a fun read."

BILL STATON
MBA, CFA, author of
Double Your Money Every Five Years
and Worry-Free Family Finances

"Ron Klein is fast becoming the 'Indiana Jones' of the fundamental truths and natural laws of success, which are universal and timeless. Because these truths and natural laws function with or without our understanding or acceptance, Ron is illuminating their truth and timeless wealth for all of us willing to take action. Ron Klein is on a mission of invitation so that we all might discover and bring to life our inherent and natural genius to create a success well within our reach that is surely enough to stagger the imagination."

MICHAEL HARRIS
MCCMaster Certified Coach with the International Coach Federation

"Turn Your Imagination into Money by Ray Giles is a rare find in a book dealing with Creativity and Imagination. It is one of those practical, self-help books that not only promises, BUT really delivers a powerful message. And, more importantly, that powerful message can be easily and successfully applied by the person who is sincere in his quest for personal achievement.

"This message on creativity is unique in itself because oftentimes individuals feel that creativity eludes them because they lack the "genius" required for the mining of rich and profitable ideas. Author Ray Giles quickly debunks this belief. Creativity and imagination can be cultivated and harvested by just changing our frame of reference. No special genes are required. No extra DNA is needed. The ability to be creative is within each of us...

..."As director of the Napoleon Hill World Learning Center at Purdue University Calumet, it is not often that I encounter a self-help book that holds my utmost attention. Too often these books are too ephemeral and lack the practicality of action oriented tasks. Not so with Ray Giles masterpiece. His book is an inspiration to the serious entrepreneur or just the ordinary person looking for a new idea or two ... Even if you've taken a course or two in creativity, I am certain that this book will reward you with some very valuable insights that you can use today as you reach for success.

It is a must read. Read it now for your personal success."

JUDY WILLIAMSON
Director of the Napoleon Hill
World Learning Center

"This book validates that we are born to use inspired ideas to solve the challenges and problems we face. Those of us who use this capacity, appear blessed, those who don't, suffer. In re-publishing "Turn Your Imagination Into Money," Ron Klein reminds us that truth is timeless and good ideas always arrive to the receptive mind."

DR. NANCY ROSANOFF
author and spiritual coach

table of contents

I | foreword

by David L. Hancock
Founder of Morgan James Publishing

EVERY day of our lives we come into contact with ideas of all kinds. Through reading, talking with others, attending seminars, and just plain thinking. Our minds process thousands of thoughts – even while we're asleep. There are enough ideas floating around to make everybody in this country successful, if we would just implement a few of them.

Often we let ideas come and go without digesting them, without acting on them or without even being aware they exist. Some of us never acquaint ourselves with great ideas in the first place. We're not in the habit of establishing a system for preserving, classifying, digesting, or using the ideas we encounter. We have no idea vault in which to save the ideas that come. The creative part of our brain starves because there are no new ideas feeding them.

One of the most important possessions a successful person has is an effective idea bank. That's the easiest way to avoid an idea shortage. A workable idea bank may be in the form of note cards or stored in binders or kept in a computer database. For example, a writer may clip newspaper articles and save them in alphabetical order according to their subject matter. That way, they can be referenced later to fill in gaps in story lines.

HOW DO WE GET IDEAS INTO OUR BANK?

It's not enough to simply write down what seem to be usable ideas. We have to learn to be systematic and uniform in our banking process.

We must first take notes, but then mix them with other ideas. Get them into our subconscious mind and put the results into a reservoir to save for later. Then finally we must implement the ideas that are immediately applicable to our situations.

The form doesn't matter. What does matter is that a logical and consistent method of retaining ideas is in place. Every successful person learns early on to warehouse their ideas somewhere, and to keep them in a form that is easy to access when they need them.

An old axiom in the newspaper business says that a good file and a poor memory are more efficient than a poor file and a good memory. It is also said that even the dullest pencil is a better instrument for preserving ideas than the sharpest memory.

ADAPTING IDEAS TO OUR SITUATIONS

Often when we get an idea, it needs to be remodeled to fit our circumstances and personality at the time. Many ideas, in fact, are stillborn to begin with, and because of lack of care, pass into oblivion before they've had a chance to develop at all. That's why we MUST get in the habit of writing ideas down. Then, when that idea's time has come, we can mold it specifically to fit our needs of the moment.

Too often people cast aside ideas that are not ready-made for them. Some of the greatest, most successful ideas in history have come about because someone was trying to develop or adapt someone else's idea. Thomas Edison proclaimed to his investors that he could develop and market a working light bulb in six weeks. It took him many months and thousands of ideas before he was successful.

And in the end, the solution had been right in front of him from the beginning. He simply would not allow that idea to fit his situation at the time, and that was almost a very costly mistake.

GIVE IDEAS EXTREME MAKEOVERS

Quite often, an idea requires an extreme makeover to be useful. Just start with the basic idea. Do some research on it to flesh it out, then think about the ideas and problems you have accumulated.

They will incubate in the depths of our minds where a workable and usable idea can be formed. The result may look something like the original idea, but produce completely different results from what you anticipated. That's okay. Ideas forged from many concepts frequently become the strongest concepts. Like metals forged from many others, they somewhat resemble the different metals they are molded from yet are often stronger than each of the original ones.

THINK BETWEEN THE LINES

Ideas can occur constantly as we get little flashes of inspiration. They come and go, often staying with us for only an instant. We must always be prepared to capture them when they come and keep a pen and paper handy at all times so we don't lose the best ones.

Once we are tuned into capturing ideas, we will get them from people, events, and circumstances all around us. When we read a book we often get more ideas from what we think between the lines than from what is actually printed in the book. That's why most publishers of learning aids put wide margins in their books – so we can write down ideas before they disappear forever!

The ideas that come to us between the lines are often more valuable than those we read in a book because they are our own. When we listen to a speech or attend a seminar, we must remember to take notes on what we hear. But also, take notes on the ideas that come to us from what we hear. Those are more than just OUR ideas, they come from divine inspiration.

SHAKE IT UP A BIT

You probably know enough about computers to realize that a disk drive without a processor is as useless as a screen door in a submarine. But put the two together; add a monitor and a program and you really have something. The same thing applies to ideas.

Alone, they may have little power or value. But mix them with other ideas and you may have a concept that can change the world.

A spark is just a spark that dissipates immediately unless you let it fall on something flammable. Then you not only have light, but you have heat and a chemical reaction. Let your ideas unite that way. Always have some paper for those little sparks to fall on. Then your idea can turn into something incredibly valuable.

Get in the habit of combining ideas and establish a research department in your head. Multiplying your efforts is like adding dynamite to that little spark of an idea. Just be careful, you might blow the roof off with the right combination!

PUT YOUR SUBCONSCIOUS TO WORK

Once you've mixed those ideas, let them tumble around in your subconscious mind. The subconscious works something like a cement mixer, constantly turning over the thoughts you've added, even while you're asleep. It can also work on ideas when you're thinking about something totally unrelated. Believe it or not, it even works when you're watching television.

A powerful set of instincts and intuitions are constantly interacting with your subconscious. Be aware of them because they also help ideas to mix. Successful people process many ideas at the same time. Thomas Edison always had people working on ideas that he came up with, no matter how unrelated the concept was to his latest project. That's how the phonograph came into being. You can do the same and experience the same results, if you'll just follow the laws of success.

BUILD AN IDEA RESERVOIR

Once you've let your subconscious mind do its work and have obtained a result you like, build a mental reservoir to put it in. This is different from an idea bank, which holds only raw and undeveloped material. While the idea is in the reservoir, related ideas and other applications of the concept will come to you.

Edison was particularly adept at developing several applications of the same idea. He already had the power plants, distribution systems and electric poles designed for his light bulbs before he ever had a working bulb. That's because he knew his basic concept was sound. It was just a matter of application.

IMPLEMENT YOUR IDEAS

When an idea is mixed thoroughly like good concrete, the time comes to put it to use. That's the final and ultimate test of an idea. Victor Hugo once said that nothing is as powerful as an idea whose time has finally arrived. An idea's time comes when you get to pour it out so that it can be used productively. Unfortunately, many people develop an idea, but stop before putting it to the final test. That's like leaving concrete in the mixer. Sooner or later it will just get hard, crack and be of no use to anyone.

TURN YOUR IMAGINATION INTO MONEY

When I founded Morgan James Publishing (with no "official" background in publishing), I was a former homebuilder and mortgage banker. I imagined that with a book I would gain more credibility in my marketplace, thus increasing my position and enable me to earn more money. That idea came from mixing my Guerrilla Marketing studies in with other ideas and out came the idea for and the book itself.

It took many years of frustration and disappointment in my initial efforts to get the book published. I eventually did get it in print and found that my income, as a mortgage banker, did in deed go up. In fact, it doubled the following year.

But I imagined that there must be a better way, and piece by piece, idea by idea, built a publishing company based on doing the opposite of what I found inadequate in the options for book publishing available at the time. I imagined a publishing company with an entrepreneurial spirit for the authors' success as well as its own.

The company that resulted is unique, even voted 44th for Fast Company Magazine's Fast50! Fast Company's fifth global readers' challenge spotlighting leading creative thinkers who have already made significant accomplishments but whose best is yet to come, and who stand to have a significant impact on the next 10 years.

Fast50 is a worldwide search for ordinary people doing extraordinary things. The goal is to remind the world of all the good that's created when passionate people with big imaginations and strong convictions are determined to make a difference.

CAN IT WORK FOR YOU?

Henry Ford had no corner on the marketing of automobiles. He simply had a concept on how to put them together cheaper, faster and more efficiently than anybody else – and he acted on that concept. He did have an advantage in that he had access to financial resources, but he did have to ACT.

Every great success in the history of man has come from the development and application of new ideas. That doesn't mean you have to create all your ideas yourself. But you do have to make them your own. You have to develop them yourself, so that you can apply them in ways that nobody else has thought of, and that can work for you. It can turn your imagination into money!

VII | ray giles and me

WE have to be open to opportunities whenever they present themselves. Often these opportunities are not unique. Many people could have taken advantage of them but didn't.

If anything, you should be encouraged by this. Too many times, when the right person comes along and seizes the opportunity, people question why it has not been done before. The public questions the validity of the venture because if it was so good, why didn't someone take advantage of the situation earlier.

A few years ago, I was reading the updated version of *Obvious Adams*. All of a sudden I read something new and exciting. It was something at least 100,000 people had read before I did.

I had just read the story of how Kraft Foods was started. At the end of the story, there was an asterisk. My eyes drifted to the bottom of the page. The asterisk indicated the story came from the book, *Turn Your Imagination Into Money!* by Ray Giles.

WOW! What a great title. I had never heard of the book or the author before. Instantly I went on the Internet and located the only copy for sale in the United States.

A few days later, I received this rare book in the mail. Ripping open the package, I devoured this long-lost treasure.

The writing was simple yet powerful. Profound. The material was refreshing. What amazed me was how timeless Giles' material was. I often got so engaged in the material that when I read Giles' mention of the −80's, I instantly thought of the 1980's. It would take a few seconds to kick in that he was referring the 1880's.

Once I finished the book, I was more confused than before. Who was Ray Giles and what else had he written? And why hadn't I heard of him before?

For the next year I purchased as many of Giles' dozen books as I could find. My first information about Giles came from his book *Breaking Through Competition*. The Blackman Company is listed under Ray's name. His later books mention Pleasantville, New York.

Pleasantville! When I first got married I lived in Pleasantville, specifically on Manville Road. It was a one bedroom condominium in a small converted garden apartment complex. We even named our first cat after Pleasantville. When I first learned about Ray Giles, I was only living about fifteen minutes away from Pleasantville.

VIII

I started researching census records from 1920 and 1930. I went to the village hall in Pleasantville. No one knew anything about this man. The Mount Pleasant Public Library had none of Ray's books. This was surprising to me at least since they were mentioned so prominently in his book *Here Comes The Band*.

I might as well have been 1500 miles from Pleasantville. Imagine, I found this great material but no one could help me learn about the author. Even though Ray Giles lived in Pleasantville, it was as though he hadn't really lived there.

Was this book still copyrighted or was it in the public domain? A thorough search showed that the author had renewed the copyright.

I felt Ray was so close yet so far away. Finally, I called one of the two funeral homes in Pleasantville to see if they had handled Ray Giles' funeral. They had and referred me to the law firm that had handled the estate. Another month or two went by. The two law partners had since split. I called the firm at the original location. I was told the records were in storage and not likely to be accessible, at least not for the foreseeable future.

When I contacted the other lawyer at his new location, he let me know his father had been Ray's attorney until his passing. Now he had handled the estate. He confirmed that the copyright had been passed on to Ray's heirs.

I now knew more. But I still didn't know how to contact Ray's heirs. I joined Ancestry.com and started to research the Giles family. Getting nowhere, I contacted the attorney in Pleasantville and asked him to contact the funeral home to learn who next of kin was or at least how to contact them in 1976 when Ray passed away.

From there I went about contacting the heirs to the estate to let them know they owned the rights to the book.

We reached an agreement to bring this classic treasure to a whole new audience. And then I was blown away. One of Ray's sons had always felt his dad's work should be reissued. Here I was contacting the Giles family a few years after the son's passing to let them know I felt the same way.

Then I found out that Ray and I had more in common than I realized. He had also lived at 289 Manville Road in Pleasantville about 17 years before I did.

Just a few thoughts before you start turning your imagination into money.

If any of the language offends you, please remember this material was written 70 years ago. The words used were in common usage at the time.

Also, while the tools and techniques we have at our disposal are significantly different today, the methods for being able to tap into our imagination have not changed. All the passage of time has done is to prove Ray Giles' wisdom is more profound than even the day he wrote it.

One final recommendation – read the book with a pen and paper handy. You never know when your imagination will reveal something so enlightening you'll want to capture it on the spot.

RON KLEIN
Chesterfield, Virginia
January 2006

TODAY many say we face a new era in business. It is comforting to remind ourselves that for centuries this prediction has been a common one. Probably the Phoenician traders talked about a "new era" when they landed first in Britain. No doubt the "new era" was a stock discussion among the toymakers of ancient Egypt. A new era in business is a chronic prospect.

But in good times or bad, whether prices rise or fall, whether optimism or pessimism prevails, one remark among business people is always so common and persistent that it fascinates me.

It is this: *"You can get the business if you have ideas!"* You hear it from the lips of the successful— from those who run tea rooms as well as from operators of huge factories, and from those who peddle safety pins from door to door or sell steam turbines to mechanical engineers, from the baker whose capital consists of a few homemade pies to the industrial leader who has millions.

Imagination has repeatedly opened the road to wealth and satisfaction for people without capital, or formal education, or apparent special ability. They made their business grow through new ideas which have often been surprisingly simple.

Webster's International Dictionary thus defines imagination:

—power or process of having mental images.

—power or process of forming ideal constructions from images, concepts, and feelings, with relative freedom from objective restraint.

—mental imaging of things not previously experienced.

—the power of the mind to decompose its conceptions, and to recombine the elements of them at its pleasure.

Looking at these definitions we realize that no one is entirely without imagination. Looking at them again, it seems possible that everyone can enlarge his ability to think creatively.

The question then arises: Is it possible for a book to help the average man or woman develop this gift of imagination?

This volume does not offer a short cut to genius. We are looking for simpler, earthier and more practical ideas than those which are likely to interest genius— ideas which appeal to everyday people and fit in with their everyday living. To be successful, every business innovation must do that.

In putting this book together I hardly know where to begin with my acknowledgments of indebtedness to others. Over a period of years, hundreds have said or done something which registered in my mind and seems worth sharing. I have been helped by competitors as well as by business partners. I owe much to clients. There are ideas here which I have received from manufacturers, bankers, mechanics, sales managers, inventors, elevator men, stenographers, iron-workers, fanners, capitalists, advertising men, and professors. It is obvious also that I am indebted to other books and to many business publications. I have tried to indicate this indebtedness without letting my text sound too much like a scrapbook of clippings. Three of my chapters are rather similar to articles which I wrote originally for Printers' Ink and Advertising and Selling.

RAY GILES New York November, 1933

1 | is originality dangerous?

chapter one

SIR ISAAC NEWTON FOUND RESISTANCE TO ORIGINAL ideas so great that he remarked a year after announcing his theory of light, "I see a man must either resolve to put out nothing new, or to become a slave to defend it."

Lombroso declared, "Man is by nature the enemy of innovation."

Benjamin Franklin's paper on "The Sameness of Lightning and Electricity," when read before the Royal Society, was met with ridicule and unbelieving laughter.

Agassiz, the great naturalist, once said: "Every great scientific truth goes through three stages. First, people say it conflicts with the Bible. Next, they say it has been discovered before. Lastly, they say they have always believed it."

The first umbrellas were condemned as attempts to interfere with God's intent that rain should fall on His children as well as on flowers, trees, and vegetables. For a similar reason the first manufacturers of baby carriages were opposed with the contention that since the Creator expressly designed feminine arms to carry infants, any attempt at substituting a labor-saving vehicle was sacrilegious.

In 1828, some young men in Lancaster, Ohio, wanted to use the school one night for a debate on the merits of the newer methods of transportation and communication. When asking permission, they stated the subject of their argument. The School Board replied: "You are welcome to the use of the school house to debate all proper questions in, but such things as railroads and telegraphs are impossible and rank infidelity. There is nothing in the word of God about them. If God had designed that His intelligent creatures should travel at the frightful speed of fifteen miles an hour by steam, He would have clearly foretold through His holy prophets. It is a device of Satan to lead immortal souls down to Hell."

Even the razor, which had been used from the days of the Pharaohs, was opposed as late as the eighties. A whole book was written which attacked shaving as unnatural and opposed to the Bible.

In face of a past like this, it is not surprising that Kenneth Goode, a present-day authority on sales promotion, believes that "man in the mass resents change and dislikes newness," "follows a habit until it hurts," and "glorifies the past and discounts the future."

BUT TIMES CHANGE

Sir Isaac Newton would find people different today. Agassiz would be delighted that the Bible is no longer quoted as an unanswerable authority against new ideas. As for Kenneth Goode, I doubt if he will discover anything in this book to which he takes exception in spite of his conviction about the innate conservatism of man in the mass.

If the new is today so unacceptable to the public, it is obvious that all industry is off on a false trail. Increasingly large sums are spent in product research. More dollars than ever before go into the testing of promising new theories about advertising and selling. Hundreds of manufacturers who have cut costs in every other direction are enlarging their expenditures for new products, new policies, new containers, and new sales promotion measures. Retailers are pinning their faith on promising new experiments. Wholesalers are fighting for existence with new ideas.

In 1931, there were 6,000 more patents granted than in 1930. In 1932, there was a further increase of 11,000 patents over 1931. It is important and significant too, that the great majority of patents granted represent simply some slight improvement in a device or product already on the market.

When we look at a roll of Kodak Verichrome film currently on sale, we find this: "Patented in U. S. A. 1,170,674 - 1,195,748 - 1,238,504 - 1,263,7541,269,365 - 1,377,158 - 1,441,146 - 1,454,8121,454,817 - 1,469,017 - 1,469,018 - 1,666,050."

Exactly how "new" is the "new" Gillette Blue Blade of 1933? That bit of steel carries this record: "Pat. Nos. 1,633,739 - 1,639,335 - 1,850,902 -1,858,316 - 1,869,327 - 1,876,906. Reissue Pat. No. 17,567. Other Pat's. Pending."

Even the plow sulky is covered by 549 different patents.

From all this we can draw one sound conclusion: when people do not respond to the new, the reason usually lies in its unfamiliarity or extreme novelty, or to doubts about its efficiency or usefulness. The plain fact is that man in the mass actually welcomes change or novelty when it is plainly an improvement over the old.

Most of us like to surround ourselves with evidence that we are modern and progressive. Imagination aimed at this trait has made overtime and night work for manufacturing plants even during periods of business depression.

"WHAT'S NEW?"

So interesting is the new that advertising writers constantly use headlines like these:

"New!" "At last-a really new..." "New Facts about..." "Now Science discovers a new way to..." "A New Sensation in..." "New Protection for your..."

The advertising man, regardless of the nature of the product or the service to be advertised, looks always for new features to emphasize. Lacking these he may even try to present the old, unchanged product in some new light. He knows from experience that stressing the new has a way of increasing sales. He never forgets that one of the commonest questions on the streets is, "What's new?"

One presidential candidate proves the value of the new by promising, if elected, a continuation of the "new era." Four years later his opponent defeats him by campaigning for a "new deal." Old barber shops, old restaurants, and even old corporations seek to revive the customer's interest and patronage by announcing themselves "Under New Management." Dying stores come back to life through new merchandise and new policies. Salesmanship thrives on "new angles" and "new approaches."

Newspapers have proved on a national scale that the man in the street has become increasingly interested in the new, even to the point of reading about abstruse scientific facts and discoveries. News about Einstein has general interest, even when it deals with what few understand. Ten years ago, the Associated Press employed no science editor and not one paper in the United States had a reporter devoting full time to science. Today the Associated Press has its science department, while many large newspapers have reporters who specialize in scientific news. More interesting still is the fact that when newspapers had to economize and cut down the space devoted to general news, few, if any, reduced their space allowance for news about medicine, astronomy, archaeology or aeronautics.

Floyd W. Parsons writes, "Whereas it took a century to develop the basic idea of Michael Faraday and from it create the electrical industry, now the same development would take place in five or six years." This belief is borne out by the fact that the automobile was accepted by the public in much less time than was the steam engine. That revolutionary new device, the radio receiving set, was accepted even more quickly than the automobile. The electric refrigerator made faster headway than the radio.

The speed with which the public accepts worthwhile new ideas is accelerating. People are passing the point where they merely accept innovation. *They are reaching the stage where they actually become indifferent to merchandise which continues year after year to be made in the same old way and put in the same old packages.* Every person who wants to make a living must give deliberate attention to the creation of practical new methods and ideas.

Fortunately, there seems to be something of a technique which almost anyone can use in developing imagination.

Hence this book.

INSIGHTS TO IMAGINATION:

One of the key statements by Giles is, "When people do not respond to the new, the reason usually lies in its unfamiliarity or extreme novelty, or to doubts about its efficiency or usefulness."

As you will see as you read more of the book, Giles will show you how to overcome the false assumptions that derail many ideas in their original form. Keeping this in mind, focus on how you can demonstrate efficiency and usefulness.

5

Take an index card and write the following: Every person who wants to make a living (or a fortune) must give deliberate attention to the creation of practical new methods and ideas. Put this card where you can see it often. It offers a great starting point to Turn Your Imagination Into Money!

7 | twenty-two springboards to imagination

chapter two

O NE JUNE NIGHT A FILLING STATION PROPRIETOR challenged his two attendants to think up some way of increasing gasoline sales. He wanted to keep both men on his payroll, but business did not warrant it. The three men thought and talked the matter over. Various possibilities were discussed. Perhaps striking signs and unusual displays would stop more passers-by; perhaps a third brand of gasoline would attract customers who might prefer it to the two already carried; perhaps inexpensive premiums given with a five or ten-gallon purchase might run up volume.

"All those ideas add to our costs," commented the boss. "I want to add business without doing that."

Finally one helper said: "Most customers ask for five gallons when often the tank will hold more. Maybe we could sell them a gallon or two more by asking, *'Shall I fill her up?'*

"This simple piece of imagination increased business about 10 percent, but some customers still replied, "Oh, I guess five gallons are enough."

Then the filling station attendant thought a step further. His object was to make it difficult for the customer to say "five gallons." A different question was tried: "How much will she hold?"

When this question was asked briskly and with the assumption that the customer wanted a full tank, his tendency was to look at the gasoline gauge and reply that the tank would hold six, eight or ten gallons, as the case might be. The attendant immediately began to pump in that amount. This idea increased sales another 10 percent.

It is good practice to think against definite problems, and an exercise which anyone can try. It is encouraging too, for anyone can get results of some kind. Never mind if your imagination seems unimportant at first: big originality is sometimes merely a little seed given a chance to grow.

H. A. Overstreet in one of his talks gave as a key to creative thinking the simple question, "Does it have to be that way?" As a light setting-up drill, this question has no equal. Take some common situation in which you find yourself. Keep thinking, "How could I improve that?" New ideas are sure to come.

Perhaps you ride to work in a trolley car. Think: "If I owned this line what could I do to improve its service and profits?" Examine every detail of the car. Think about the people who ride in it what changes would make their ride more pleasant without adding expense? Think of the transportation line as a whole; if you do this you will begin to get ideas like these: The windows will not open easily and the ride would be pleasanter on hot days if that difficulty were removed. Some redesigning of the seats might make them more comfortable. And so on.

Another day, as you are walking along the street, imagine that you own a store. Consider what you would do to make it more attractive. Look at the different store fronts. Notice the colors used; you will be surprised to see how little originality is displayed in painting stores. Note the sameness of lettering on the signs and the sameness of window displays. Think what you could do to make your store more attractive to the eye. Then try this exercise on different types of stores in turn- specialty shops, drug stores, hardware stores, etc.

I went to the automobile show one year with a man who was fond of exercises of this kind. His comments on the new cars were interesting. Coming to one of the best sellers, he said: "I think they will have to modify that radiator inside of a year; it's too extreme for the public." His prediction came true. Stopping in front of another car which had adopted a radical new design, he remarked: "That whole car is a dangerous experiment. It will be interesting to see if it sells at all." Within a few months, the manufacturer of the car went into bankruptcy.

The ability to think practical, original ideas is latent in all of us. We all see something at times which we think could be done better. Anyone can imagine a house, an automobile, or an animal with new features in it. Perhaps these features will be impractical, but through continued exercise of this sort one's ideas will grow better and better. Finally, we may develop judgment as good as that of the friend who went with me to the automobile show.

"Originality," declares T. W. Higginson, "is simply a pair of fresh eyes." We can cultivate the habit of looking at things as though we never before saw them. Then start thinking about improvements. Keep looking, looking, looking. Constantly, we must look for and consider differences as well as likenesses.

As a help to developing originality and imagination, this chapter contains twenty-two springboards to new ideas, all of which have proved their value many times.

Borrow from Nature. Nature is one of the most important sources of new ideas. One who knows anatomy realizes that the human body contains suggestions useful in mechanical invention. The idea for the lasso is in the spider's web. Fish and flowers suggest unusual and beautiful color combinations which may be borrowed for packages, store fronts, color advertising, and dress goods. Nature also supplies patterns for textiles and wall paper. Gothic architecture was inspired by the pine forests.

Borrow from the Past. When a thing becomes old enough it can be revived sometimes as new. Thus two advertising slogans used by one of the big cigarette manufacturers were shown to be suspiciously like slogans used years ago for a popular patent medicine. In the Metropolitan Museum of Art is an ancient wheeled toy which might have inspired the Kiddie Kar. When ordnance experts wanted to design helmets and side arms for soldiers in the World War, they found it useful to study the collection of ancient armor in the Metropolitan.

Borrow from Abroad. Many popular food specialties are borrowed from abroad. Junket, for example. An American watched Mexican natives making crackers and he commercialized the idea with great success in this country. The beer garden, the coffee house, the cafe, the rathskeller all are imported ideas.

Borrow from other Industries. The idea for the cash register came to Jacob Ritty, a Dayton merchant, while he watched a device recording propeller revolutions on an Atlantic steamship. He saw that this mechanical device might be adapted to register the amount of money in a till.

Dissect to Know Details. While still a railroad man, Walter Chrysler bought an automobile just to take it apart and learn how it worked. He thought up improvements too, for his first Chrysler car was the admiration of engineers. Dissect your gift shop, your job as floorwalker, your cement factory. How can you build improvements into it? Children learn by taking things apart; adults can profit by their example.

Ask Customers for their Ideas. A boot manufacturer makes a trip each year among farmers, asking their ideas about footwear. The manufacturer of an ointment, during some house-to-house visits with consumers, found that users did not like the stain left by his product and so he made it colorless and non-staining.

Work over One Detail after Another. One original man says he does this because even little betterments may lead to greater sales.

It is easier, too, than trying to change a whole plan or product. A developer of real estate increases his sales through little differences in the houses he builds. He may erect twenty houses which are much alike; but one has flower boxes in the front windows, another has an especially good garage, a third may have two fine apple trees out front, while a fourth has an unusually attractive fireplace.

Focus Thought on Weak Spots. A tobacconist sold more cigarettes by packing some in sandalwood boxes which gave the tobacco a distinctive flavor. Some years ago a lawyer took over a hosiery factory and raised it to leadership by his determination that socks should have stronger toes, heels, and soles. By putting a crinkle into hairpins another manufacturer made a new kind which stayed in the hair better. By roughening his paper clips, another manufacturer made them hold papers together more securely, and he is said to have made a million dollars from this one small innovation.

Imagine Your Present Market Wiped Out. This exercise led a manufacturer of marshmallows to introduce a three-pound package for the kitchen. The marshmallows inside were used for cakes and cookies. An automobile horn with slight alteration was sold also as a factory signal. A maker of alarm clocks found that he could also sell clockworks for use in mechanical toys. Timothy Dexter, an early New England merchant, sent a shipment of warming pans to Cuba where the captain found that sugar planters welcomed them to skim impurities off boiling sugar. Another enterprising trader sent baby's cradles to California during the gold rush of '49, where the miners used them as rockers in mining gold.

11

Look to Hobbies. Perhaps your hobby might be turned into a vocation more profitable than your present work. Amateur golf players have made money by becoming professionals. One man collected butterflies as a boy; now he makes a living by selling butterflies by mail.

You may make money by catering to the hobbies of others. The manufacturer of a chocolate candy made extra sales to boys by enclosing a foreign postage stamp with each bar. During the nineties Ivory soap featured in one of its advertisements the parties then common where men and women amused themselves by blowing bubbles from clay pipes. Of recent years, tons of Ivory Soaps have been whittled away by amateur sculptors who carve it into little figures.

Two Old Ideas may be United into One New One. Did you ever look at a chair and wonder what added touch would open some new market? One man added a tilting device and a cuspidor and thus invented the dentist's chair. Another built extra width into one arm which made a chair useful for taking notes in a lecture hall and good, also, to hold an egg sandwich and a cup of coffee in a lunch room. A razor plus a protective guard made a fortune.

Experiment even with the Useless. Over-burned and under-burned bricks were once thrown away but one day some one tried building them into a wall. The varicolored effect was pleasing. The former discards were rechristened "Tapestry Bricks" and were easily sold at a premium. Cypress with worm holes was discarded until an experimentalist found that it made handsome woodwork.

Stuff up on your Subject. Read everything you can find. Ask people their opinions. Enlarge the borders of your general knowledge. "Wealth of ideas is closely related to the number of words used to express them. In 1928 Webster's unabridged dictionary contained 70,000 words. The latest edition lists more than 400,000."

Experiment with Appearance. Some time, if you want to give an imagination party, make each guest draw a new kind of automobile, a new kind of house. Have the members of your family try it, too. What can you do with color alone? Through wrapping paper of an unusual color, a store adds to its individuality; by dressing waitresses in odd colors, a tea room makes itself remembered.

Try "Fool's Experiments". The cocktail was an accident, resulting from tasting one day some odds and ends which had been thrown into an empty vessel in a barroom. Ice cream was invented accidentally through placing a creamy dessert in an icy mountain pool— when they went to get it they had something original.

How can you prolong your selling season or increase your usefulness? Coca-Cola, once a summer drink, is now popular also in winter. Ice cream sells increasingly in winter. Those summer BVD's were so comfortable that many men discarded winter underwear to wear BVD's the year around. A metropolitan hotel now advertises special room rates for day use, and women shoppers from the suburbs appreciate the convenience and opportunity to freshen up. The early automobiles were impossible in winter; economical enclosed bodies had to come before cars were used the year through. Banks increase deposits by providing outside slots through which bank books can be thrust together with deposits. A shoe store in a big city enjoys additional business by remaining open all night.

Cater to a Special Group. Some specialize in making garments for stout women. There are shoe manufacturers who specialize in shoes for feet with weak arches. A department store attracts small boys by housing a barber shop where they can sit on hobby horses while their hair is being cut. The A & P built a huge chain of general grocery stores through a start which specialized in tea, coffee, and spices.

13

Think Ten Years Ahead. In his mind's eye, Henry Ford could see Woodward Avenue in Detroit crowded with automobiles, and every family eager to own a car. That spurred him into making the dream come true. Experienced real estate men can look at bare acreage, see ten years ahead, and tell you where the houses ought to be. How about your own work? What changes do you think will come in the next ten years? How far can you anticipate these changes and do something about them?

What Related Activity will help? Today Western Union boys deliver many things beside telegrams. They deliver orange juice, sandwiches and other goods sold by a chain. They have been hired by manufacturers to distribute samples of toothpaste, bread, magazines, books, and shaving cream. All this related activity makes more profits for the Western Union and more jobs for boys.

Every week over 400,000 housewives get a four-page pamphlet from the A & P containing budgeting suggestions about feeding a family of four. Menus for different meals are suggested-a related activity that sells more groceries.

What Laboratory Products may be Commercialized? Saccharin was only a chemical curiosity until some one found that it could be substituted for sugar in the diets of diabetics. The thermos bottle was made originally for use in laboratories.

What Change of Ingredients might Lead to Something New? A steel vacuum bottle sells at a higher price because glass bottles break. Steel tennis rackets and fishing poles compete successfully with wooden ones.

What Possession have You that Might be Turned into a Business? A man in Vermont designed a vehicle for his boy and it swept the country later as the Kiddie Kar. Another man in East Medway, Mass., had an exceptionally fine spring on his farm. In the early eighties ginger ale was imported, and Lansing Millis, who owned the farm, liked the English ginger ale. In addition to the spring he had a small bottling plant for cider. He decided that the water from his spring might be used for a superior ginger ale. Ultimately he brought out Clicquot Club Ginger Ale which made him wealthy. A Westerner who raised goats to supply milk for his daughter found that others also preferred it to cow's milk; now he has a herd of ninety nannies, makes daily delivery of goat's milk to every part of the city, and has a very profitable business.

But in using these springboards to originality, remember that your ideas must be geared in with actual needs and creatable wants of real people. Ralph Waldo Emerson learned that when he left New England to go West. There he found the people quite unlike those he had known in the East, and he had to humanize his academic talks to make them popular. Out of this experience, he made this observation: "It is necessary that you should know the people's facts. If you have no place for them, the people absolutely have no place for you."

INSIGHTS TO IMAGINATION:

Think of your daily life. Try to apply Haring's question, *"Does it have to be that way?"* at least 5 times a day. Go for a walk and apply it. If you stop at a convenience store in the morning, look around you. What would you do differently to improve the store?

Just as the two gas attendants asked questions that increased sales, what questions could you ask customers or potential customers to increase your business without increasing cost? The famous line "would you like fries with that" which has evolved into a meal or sandwich has made McDonalds untold millions of dollars in additional revenue. How many times have you placed an order at a fast food restaurant and the person behind the register says, "Is that all?" You most likely said yes and were done with your order. If they had a little more courtesy and asked if there anything else you would like, you might have ordered more. And if they had made a suggestion, you might have spent even more.

Think about questions the next time you go to the Post Office. Regardless of what brought you, there is one question you will always be asked – "Do you need stamps today?"

Is there a "would you like fries with that" or "do you need stamps today" question you can ask in your business? If you are thinking of starting a business, this exercise can help you build sales right from the beginning.

BORROW FROM NATURE

Velcro™ was created from a walk through brush. The gentleman who created it was intrigued by the way burrs stuck to his wool trousers. Upon looking at the burrs under magnification,

15

he noticed they had hooks which got caught on the loops of his wool pants. Out of this observation came Velcro™.

BORROW FROM THE PAST

Chainmail was often used in medieval times to prevent knights in battle from being cut by sharp objects. Scuba divers diving in shark infested waters use a wet suit incorporating chainmail to protect them from shark bites. If you watch a professional shuck oysters, you soon realize they are wearing a glove made of chainmail.

BORROW FROM ABROAD

If you go back for the past thirty years or so and analyze some of the top television shows, you realize a great many of them were either copied or adapted from England.

"All in the Family" was adapted from "Until Death Us Do Part"; "Sanford and Son" from "Steptoe and Son".

"Who Wants to be a Millionaire" was first a British game show. The extremely popular "Antiques Roadshow" started in Great Britain and was later brought over here airing on PBS.

FOCUS ON WEAK SPOTS

The example Ray Giles used about the reinforced socks was reintroduced some twenty years ago and launched as the gold toe line. Again, strengthening key areas of socks was considered new all over again.

IMAGINE YOUR PRESENT MARKET WIPED OUT

When I was a child, parents thought nothing of giving their children baby aspirin. Later on it was discovered that aspirin caused Reyes Syndrome. The market for this over the counter analgesic was essentially wiped out. Now children's aspirin is recommended for adults to take once daily to prevent heart attacks.

LOOK TO HOBBIES

Many businesses have been started from hobbies. Mrs. Fields started her cookie empire from the positive response her cookies generated from her friends and family. Magnetic Poetry started out as a way to inspire creativity for a frustrated songwriter fighting off allergies. Now their products can be found everywhere.

EXPERIMENT WITH THE USELESS

Before 1964 chicken wings didn't offer much value to anyone. Then one night in 1964 in Buffalo, New York, one creative woman cooked up a combination that sells wings all over the world. Chicken wings now sell at a premium in both restaurants and supermarkets.

Do you have a product that is not perfect but is sold in a different form for a new use? Broken cookies or candy bars for example are sold to yogurt and ice cream manufacturers to be used as mix-ins.

Review these 22 springboards for inspiration. Focus on one or two at a time. You'll be amazed at the results you get.

chapter three

People were fond of calling Burbank a "plant wizard." To the man himself any suggestion that his success resulted from anything but normal powers was unwelcome. Burbank was an able business man in addition to being a creative botanist. Over and over he proved his ability to solve the unusual business problems which occurred in his work. As a young man he did not stand out among his fellows. "On the contrary," we read in a biographical sketch, "he was rather below the average size and not at all robust. He worked in a plow factory for fifty cents a day, clerked in a furniture store, and started out to study medicine. Then a long siege of ill health, caused by sunstroke, overtook him; and in 1875 he went to California to regain his strength and to acquire a seed farm." He saved the larger part of his wages so that he might own a nursery of his own.

WANTED 20,000 PRUNE TREES

Three years passed before Burbank's first great chance came. An impatient fruit grower was visiting one nursery after another to secure 20,000 prune trees. As though the order itself were not staggering enough, he coupled it with a stiff requirement: the trees must be delivered ready for planting within ten months. "Impossible," said one nurseryman after another. Out at Santa Rosa, Burbank heard about the order and went after it. The prune trees had to be started immediately, but prunes wouldn't sprout at that time of the year. To make a beginning, Burbank planted almonds and then came the demand for an "infinite capacity for taking pains." Burbank had to select special soil. He had to cover the germinated almonds with cloth, and as they poked their green spikes above the earth he had to remove them one at a time to nursery rows. Twenty thousand almond trees couldn't go wrong.

Next he needed prune buds with which to work his 20,000 miracles. When the young almond trees were well along, the prune buds were grafted into them. The tops of the young trees were broken off to force new growth. In less than seven months, Luther Burbank delivered 19,025 prune trees ready for planting. Let us look closer at this combination of creative thought and action. Some of the characteristics we observe are these:

Willingness to attempt the impossible. A famous scientist admits, "I no longer call anything impossible because in days past when I used to do so, some darned fool always came along to prove me wrong." An equally prominent business man explains his phenomenal success by saying, "We fired the men who refused to attempt the impossible."

Intense concentration. Burbank, himself, declared: "The average man rarely sets the undivided force of his mind to work on a single task continuously. He thinks of the automobile he is going to buy, the show he is going to see, or the raise he thinks he ought to have."

No worship of past or present. The fact that there was no precedent to make the feat seem possible had no weight with Luther Burbank.

Consecration. To his intense mental concentration, Burbank added the willingness to work night and day to achieve his result.

Faith. Burbank had faith both in his unusual idea as to how the trees could be grown and in his ability to put that plan into action. No doubt he realized the truth summed up so well by Professor A. N. Whitehead: "It is no paradox to say that in our most theoretical moods, we may be nearest to our most practical application."

Range of knowledge. Did any of the other nurserymen see the possibility of growing prune trees from almonds? No doubt many of them stopped short at the conclusion that it was the wrong time of the year to plant prune trees. While the man whose whole working life is spent at one lathe may get ideas which improve that machine, the creative mind usually has a wide range of information and its interests spread out in many directions. Burbank did not give up when he realized that the season was wrong for growing prune trees. He went right on to the next step, "but almond trees can be started now and I can graft prune buds to them later!"

Daring. Burbank gave evidence of this quality by going straight ahead on a large scale. His investment in supplies and time must have been large. Failure would have entailed serious loss.

Persistence— obviously a necessity for anyone who must do so much manual work before the trees would be ready for delivery.

As we look at other creative minds at work, or recall our own experiences in creative thinking, we will remember that the inventive mind includes still other characteristics: —observation —expectancy —exhilaration —self-forgetfulness —forgetfulness of surroundings —intentness on a goal —active thought and quiet reflection in alteration and proper balance —thought turned into sustained action and carried through to a conclusion.

If we examine again these characteristics, we find that none seem beyond the reach of the average man. They are all qualities that can be cultivated. Burbank himself held this belief: "It is not difficult to start in business and to make the business profitable. The mainsprings of business success, in my opinion, are concentration and persistence. It has been proved time and again that the normal man has in him the latent capacity for far greater things than he accomplishes in his daily routine. It is only a question of arousing this capacity and establishing the habit of putting it to its best uses constantly."

INDIRECT SUCCESS

Professor Whitehead cautions us emphatically against fear of our theoretical moods. Why? One reason is that "wild" ideas are often rich in practical possibilities. Edison and Darwin showed a willingness to play with "fool's experiments" because

(1) Every experiment enlarges the experimenter's knowledge;

(2) A certain percent of the experiments are bound to bear fruit.

One of the most inventive merchants in the Middle West gives this advice: "When you have a business problem, get out a pad and let your mind run along at random. Set down every possible answer that comes to you, no matter how silly it may seem to be at the time. Don't stop to analyze the value of each idea, just continue to put down more thoughts. Then review what you have. If you still haven't secured the best answer, go at it again the next day. If your experience is anything like mine, you will be astonished at the ease with which new ideas come." The point under consideration here is that our best ideas are not always the first to come. One man who has become wealthy through his ability to get new ideas makes it a rule to hunt for answers to problems even after he has one that seems to be more than ordinarily good. This practice taps our subconscious reservoirs and brings out the best we have in us.

Every "fool's experiment" is worth while. Consider the case of Henry Ford. At one time in his youth he planned a watch factory to be run by himself and some friends. It would produce 2,000 timepieces a day. At one end of the plant the raw materials would enter; at the other they would emerge as finished watches. Supplies would be bought in huge quantities and costs would be so low that a good watch could be made for only 37 cents and sold for half a dollar. Ford never gave the world 50-cent watches, but it is clear that his "fool's experiment" in thinking was not wasted. It bobbed up later in another industry and at a time when he had the riper experience to put it to work. That is like aiming at a crow and bringing down an eagle.

ALWAYS AT THE LEARNING POINT

Some years ago, one of my most valued coaches in originality told me one day about a train ride he had with another executive who was prominent at the time. "But he won't last long" my friend declared; "I talked with him for three hours straight and he didn't ask a single question." This lack of the inquiring mind my coach regarded as a sure sign of mental letdown. It turned out that he was right; a year later the man who did not need to ask any more questions was replaced by some one else. The creative mind constantly looks for new information, new experiences, and new fields for speculation. It retains always something of the attitude of Laplace, the great astronomer. At 78 he died, crying out, "What we know is nothing; what we do not know is immense."

We should keep our eyes on the laboratories, too. Here are the beginnings of new industries and new vocations. Not so long ago the steam turbine was nothing but a laboratory toy. Sir James Dewar in his experiments with liquefied gases perfected a device for retaining these in their liquid state. It was this container which others commercialized as the Thermos or vacuum bottle, a laboratory vessel converted into a bottle which keeps hot drinks hot and cold drinks cold.

We should be interested in nature. Observations of animal and plant life have led to many important discoveries. Igo Etrich says that he got the idea for his Taube airplane from the seed of the zanonia, a vine which he saw in India. The shape suggested a new design which made the Taube one of the most efficient flying machines of its day. Certain questions about the phenomena connected with volcanic eruptions were solved by d'Orbigny when he was watching a peasant woman one day as she ironed clothes.

As she spit on the iron to test its heat, he noticed that the saliva flew off the hot surface before it could evaporate. That started a chain of thought which cleared up some questions that had long puzzled scientists.

Finally, we should be endlessly curious about everything that pertains to the work we like best, for that is where we have our greatest natural aptitude and stand the best chance of achieving both distinction and financial success.

INSIGHTS TO IMAGINATION:

One of the key components of having a creative attitude is asking questions of yourself and others. Make it a practice to ask questions as often as possible. The learning opportunities are endless.

Giles writes, "Finally, we should be endlessly curious about everything that pertains to the work we like best, for that is where we have our greatest natural aptitude and stand the best chance of achieving both distinction and financial success."

Review the story of Luther Burbank. The key to his success was combining thought and action. If he had just had the creative inspiration and stopped right there, would he have had success? If he had just taken action without thought, would he have had success? It's doubtful.

25 | the archaelogical viewpoint
and other obstacles to originality

chapter four

O VER IN ONE OF THE EAST INDIES, THE PEOPLE FILE THEIR teeth down to the gums. When a Caucasian visitor asked why, he was told, "Always so have done." The idea that a thing is right because "always so have done" is one of the greatest hindrances to the development of originality; indeed, some believe it is the only really important obstacle.

A friend who is internationally known as the originator of new varieties of flowers and fruits, tells me that when a young man he was undecided as to which science he would make his life calling. Finally he narrowed down to two alternatives: He would be either a botanist or an archaeologist. He says, "I chose botany because in archaeology you are always looking at the past." No doubt this gentleman would have achieved distinction as an archaeologist, but he would never have had the creative satisfaction that has come to him in the field he chose. He did not make his choice for financial reasons, but today if he wished to use his science for money-making only, his forward-looking viewpoint and creative experience in botany could be capitalized either in growing for the market or in the origination of new varieties. It is not so easy to capitalize a serious backward-looking subject like archaeology. For every one person who goes to Egypt to admire the past, there are probably a thousand who prefer Paris and its modern night life.

If we want to develop imagination we cannot afford to be archaeologists. The constant search for precedents, together with study of legal decisions made in years gone by, has a deadening effect on lawyers as a group. Some think it explains why the originality of the legal profession falls below that of business men, doctors, and architects. The lawyer must be an archaeologist during part of his time whether he likes it or not. Any locomotive designer who frequently had to study steam engines of the past would probably find his originality drying up too.

It is true that all of us must know something of the past; we cannot discard its lessons entirely. The gentleman who preferred botany to archaeology was willing enough to profit by the work done by Linnaeus and others. But he used knowledge accumulated in centuries gone by as a springboard into the new and that is about all the past is good for.

Some businesses must cling to the past more than others. A hot dog stand can launch striking new ideas more readily than an insurance company. We expect conservatism from our bank but not from our favorite filling station. The treasurer of a company is quite properly more of an archaeologist than is the sales promotion manager. A salesman may need to experiment and throw over old practices from day to day, but a factory foreman cannot do so without the risk of running costs up dangerously. However, fear to quit the past can easily be fatal to originality. There are other obstacles, too. Let us look at some of them. How about this one?

"I'M NOT CLEVER AT ALL!"

Even great geniuses are not always clever. Edison had no formal education; he was even contemptuous of college training. His skull was so unusual in shape that the family doctor shook his own head doubtfully and predicted "brain trouble." At school, Edison lagged along consistently near the foot of the class and after three months he was dismissed as being too stupid to go on. The teacher called him "addled". After that, all of Edison's schooling came from his mother. Luther Burbank, whose 20,000 prune trees started him off toward fame, did not stand out from his fellows when he was young. Apparently he did not shine in either the plow factory or the furniture store where he worked.

Havelock Ellis has made an extended study of genius. After reviewing the histories of hundreds of superior minds, he found that, while there was a tendency to precociousness, even the outstanding genius seemed to reach his full powers later in life than the average person. It does not appear that cleverness, as we ordinarily think of it, is at all necessary for sound creative thinking.

"I'M NOT WELL EDUCATED"

B. C. Forbes has gathered some interesting information about the early lives of successful businessmen. The omission of advanced education in many cases is conspicuous.

Robert Dollar, founder of a big steamship line, was a cook's boy.

W. L. Douglas, the shoe man, pegged footwear. James B. Duke, tobacco king, peddled leaf tobacco.

T. Coleman duPont was a coal miner. George Eastman was an insurance clerk. Thomas Edison was a newsboy. James A. Farrell was a laborer. Henry Ford was a machinist. Darwin P. Kingsley was a farm hand. John H. Patterson was a toll collector. John D. Rockefeller clerked in an office. Charles M. Schwab was a grocery clerk.

F. W. Woolworth worked on a farm.

This list might be extended through many pages, but from these few examples it would appear that conventional education is not essential to creative thinking.

"BUT I'M ACTUALLY DUMB"

A shipping clerk who held this low opinion of himself was told to try an experiment. He was to stare as vacantly as he liked at the crates and boxes that left his department every day. On

Monday he was to keep thinking, "How could they be made to look better without increasing the cost?" On Tuesday he moved on to "Could they be made stronger without adding either to the weight or the cost?" On Wednesday he shifted over to "Could the boxes be simplified without losing strength?" On Thursday, "Could they be made to do something that they don't do now?"

We will stop at that point because on Thursday the shipping clerk's imagination began to function. He says: "I got to thinking about the boxes and all the people who handle them before they are finally chopped up for kindling wood. I thought that we could just as easily print a ten-word selling talk on the side along with our name. Then when the truckman takes the boxes away from the factory, he knows not only what we make but how good it is. The same goes for the men who load the boxes on the trains. Then another truckman takes the stuff to the wholesaler's. It does no harm to keep repeating to the wholesaler and his people the reason why our stuff is easy to sell. The selling talk on the box would be a reminder, also, to the people in the stores that sell our line. Finally the box is chopped up and the fellow with the ax learns about us, too. Or maybe some kid gets the box and makes it into a body for his cart and thus displays the selling talk all over town. Wouldn't that be swell?"

The shipping clerk's idea was fresh and perfectly sound. The $7,000 advertising manager and the $10,000 sales manager admitted that they should have thought of it themselves, and that pleased the shipping clerk immensely. He decided that he had been dumb by choice and not by necessity.

"I HAVEN'T THE TIME"

Herbert Spencer rarely worked more than three hours a day. Darwin, when busy with The Origin of Species, worked usually from 8 A.M. until 9:30 and then from 10:30 through noon. After a session of this sort, he often said, "I've done a good day's work." J. P. Morgan commonly quit work at 3:30 P.M. A famous railway magnate spends most of his mornings in bed. So while we have our Edisons who can work day after day with practically no sleep, they are the exceptions. One sales executive had become so immersed in detail that he no longer had time to think creatively about sales expansion. He was advised to take three half hours a week and devote them entirely to thinking up new ways to get more business. He took his half hour on Monday, Wednesday, and Friday, and made his appointments and the day's mail allow him that freedom. He soon found this hour and a half a week more profitable than any of his days spent solely in management.

As a matter of fact, few of us are so engaged that we must keep our minds at concert pitch for even five hours a day. If we cannot find half an hour a day for creative thinking, we are poor managers and ought to do something about it. Instead of looking on thinking as so much more hard work added to the day's labors, we can anticipate it with even greater eagerness than time spent in piecing together a jigsaw puzzle or playing bridge.

"I HAVEN'T THE RIGHT SURROUNDINGS"

By this, the complainer usually means that he hasn't a special soundproof study, the intellectual stimulation of brilliant friends and associates, or some other environmental factor which he thinks necessary for the production of new ideas. Such excuses are not valid.

The most stimulating environment for creative thinking in business is right on the firing line-face to face with the public. The best advertising ideas come not from going into a trance, but from talking with typical consumers to get at first hand their thoughts about the product to be advertised. The best selling talks are not sermonettes worked out in the solitude of a private office, but simple messages developed from trying one approach after another on living customers. The best product innovations are got out among users, finding out what they like and dislike. In business, our starting point is always people— when we are among people we are in the right surroundings, and no one needs to spend money to make contacts with customers.

"BUT I CAN'T SEEM TO GET THE VIEWPOINT OF OTHERS OR SYMPATHIZE WITH IT"

If you are too self-centered, you may need extra contact with the kind of people at whom your business thinking must be directed. One advertising manager makes it a rule to clerk two weeks a year in a typical store selling his product. A shoe manufacturer tells me that he maintains a shoe store under another name in a large city where he goes periodically to sit at the feet of his customers so that he may keep alive the common touch. If, after efforts of this kind, you simply can't get the "feel" of the average man, you may have to redirect your aim to some smaller group within the consuming public. Plenty of fortunes have been made from comparatively few customers. Unless you are a rare person indeed, there is some group of people with whom you can feel in sympathy— it may be the "class" market, the high-school boys, the Methodists, the firemen, those of Italian descent, or some other section of the public.

"I'M TOO LAZY"

"If there is a devil in you, put him to work," advised Elbert Hubbard. If there is a lazy cuss in you, he, too, can be turned to a purpose. It may help to realize that your laziness is entirely normal. Dr. Paul Nystrom points out that we have become a nation of sitters and we seem to like it. More housework is done in a sitting position than ever before; even the farmer is doing more of his work from the seat of a machine. We take our sports while sitting as spectators, rising only occasionally for a stretch. My son and I passed a neighbor's house lately and saw the maid sitting on a chair in the living room while pushing the vacuum cleaner over the floor; the rest of her sat there limp and lazy. We prefer a seat in an automobile to a brisk walk over the hills. Think up new ways to satisfy your own desire to be lazier still! How can you make matters easier for yourself and others? How can you make that package easier to open? How can you make that advertisement so effective that you can repeat it over and over again and not have to prepare three new pieces of copy every week? What can you say in ten minutes that will sell your goods to a customer so effectively that you can have more time for loafing?

"I'M NOT PHYSICALLY UP TO PAR"

This may be a valid excuse, but does your doctor agree? Even if he thinks you have handicaps, he may be wrong. Poor physical condition does not always weigh down heavily on thinking ability. Few people manage to avoid physical defects, and even the prize-winning babies hardly ever approach 100 percent perfection.

One famous business authority was a consumptive and had to plan his office so that he could be in the open air, summer and winter. Others manage active business lives, including plenty of original thinking, with defective hearts, kidneys, or whatever else it is that may trouble people. Two men who have made at least a million dollars apiece through original thinking are subject to frequent and incapacitating headaches.

"I'M TOO YOUNG OR TOO OLD"

This obstacle has been covered by others so well and so often that it hardly needs discussion here. The period between 20 and 40 years of age appears to be most favorable to creative thinking. But the only reason why 18 doesn't ordinarily shine is that he hasn't yet had the experience, while 62 tapers off because his mind has "jelled" and he has too many set ideas or is too fond of the good old ways.

"I HAVE AN INFERIORITY COMPLEX"

Good! Cling to it, for it forces you to set high standards for yourself. Lacking confidence, you must keep on thinking until your ideas are well above customary standards. Only when you have something extraordinarily good do you gain confidence enough to make it public. Some of the best salesmen are actually bashful, but they succeed because bashfulness forces them to represent only goods in which they have a deep belief. Then, also,

31

their superior intelligence compels them to sell in a restrained way and from the customer's standpoint. Compared to the over-confident salesmen, they are real builders of business. So don't be ashamed of your diffidence; superior intelligence usually goes with bashfulness.

"I LIKE THE OLD WAYS BEST!"

That seems to bring us around again to where this chapter started. "I like the old ways best" means "I prefer to be an archae-ologist." Well, even an archaeologist can get more fun out of his expeditions if he thinks up new methods of uncovering ruins and new ways of preserving old palaces and temples.

INSIGHTS TO IMAGINATION:

Do you look at your business or ideas as an archaeologist would? If you get caught up in precedent and what was done previously, how can you turn that around to look toward the future?

Give yourself or someone who works for you the same assign-ment the shipping clerk completed. Pick a specific part of your product or service. If the answers don't come on the first day don't worry. Just keep the creative flow going and enjoy the results.

One of the best things you can do for yourself is to create the three half hours weekly for creative thinking. Make certain you are away from your normal business distractions so your creative mind is free to roam. The only tools you will need are paper and pen and the ability to let go.

I'M TOO LAZY

Giles tells of the maid who vacuumed sitting on a chair. There is now a robotic vacuum that doesn't require us to do anything. That idea has also been adapted to a robotic lawn mower. So, if you choose, you can have your carpets vacuumed and your lawn mowed from the comfort of your couch.

Think of the last container of milk or orange juice you opened. Chances are you unscrewed a plastic cap and pulled off the protective cover. Realize how much easier that was than the days of pulling the carton apart and sticking your fingers in to try to peel the layers from each other.

There are tremendous opportunities and profits to be realized by appealing to people's desire for laziness.

33

35 | how can we get new ideas?

H. A. HARING STOOD IN THE DOOR OF MY OFFICE. Haring has national standing as an authority on warehousing; in addition, he is a sound and fertile adviser on other business problems. After we greeted each other, he said, "I don't see how you can do any thinking here." That rather surprised me, for I considered my working quarters close to ideal. The office was high on a twenty-sixth floor, and the noise from the street was not bothersome. As the room was on a corner, I had light from two sides. My secretary sat in a connecting room so that neither her typewriter nor her telephone calls could bother me.

The office seemed quiet and private to me, but my visitor, coming down from the Catskills, had another ideal in mind. He heard plenty of noise from the streets below. My telephone interruptions, though few, were numerous enough in his opinion to nip any budding inspiration. And three people poked their heads into my office during the few minutes that passed before we went out.

At lunch, Haring explained that for years he operated under conditions beside which mine were as quiet as a cemetery. His work started ahead of breakfast, for even before he could enjoy his rolls and coffee he had to make out-of-town telephone calls to plan his day. As he described his operations, I realized that he matched in real life those pictures of super-executives which we see in the movies. Then Haring made a complete change. He left the Middle West and came east to settle down in a Catskill village. He travels the country as the need arises, but most of his creative thinking is done in the mountains. And he says that he gets further with it there than he ever did in an office. He related an experience which bore out his belief.

A nationally famous executive arrived at his place in the Catskills late one Friday afternoon with a problem that had perplexed him for weeks. He had motored over two hundred miles to have an evening's consultation. His plan was that they would discuss the problem through to a conclusion before bedtime and then he would head for home. Haring took the chauffeur aside and told him to drive to the next village, put up there and return on Sunday afternoon. The two men then sat down to think the problem over, but the visitor was too tense to think straight— he had been at the problem too steadily. Midnight came and he learned that he would have to remain overnight. He didn't relish the enforced detention, but he took his prescription, which was to let go, relax, and get again into prime thinking condition. Most of Saturday was passed in the garden. On Sunday or perhaps it was late Saturday night the client said suddenly: "Why I've got the answer. And it's simple. I wonder why I didn't think of it before."

This is a good story, because most of us have had similar experiences. It suggests several points in developing a technique of going after new ideas. One point is that usually it does not pay to keep churning away too steadily at a problem; even when the problem is an urgent one, alternation of work and play may bring a better and quicker solution. This is a familiar piece of wisdom, but many business people quite thoroughly disregard it. In my own case, I put Haring's story to use shortly after. I had a problem that I wanted to solve in five hours flat. At my office I steeped myself in the details for an hour. Then I went to the library of one of New York's largest hotels which is about the quietest place I know of in that city. I read a copy of the South African Gazette quite deliberately, and as though I had all the time in the world at my disposal. Then I took up the problem again and a good solution came through in less than thirty minutes.

VERIFICATION FROM HELMHOLTZ

Graham Wallas, in *The Art of Thought*, tells us that Helmholtz, the famous German physicist, in speaking at a banquet on his seventieth birthday explained his success at creative thinking. He said that after thorough investigation of a problem "in all directions... happy ideas came unexpectedly without effort, like an inspiration. So far as I am concerned, they never came to me when my mind was fatigued, or when I was at my working table.... They came particularly readily during the slow ascent of wooded hills on a sunny day."

Wallas analyzes this process. He points out that we have here three stages in the formation of a new idea. "The first in time I shall call Preparation, the stage during which the problem was 'investigated... in all directions'; the second is the stage during which he was not consciously thinking about the problem, which I shall call Incubation; the third, consisting of the appearance of the 'happy idea' together with the psychological events which immediately preceded and accompanied that appearance, I shall call Illumination.... And I shall add a fourth stage, of Verification, which Helmholtz does not here mention."

This analysis is well worth repeating:

(1) Preparation through investigation;
(2) Incubation, a rest period when the mind is devoted to other matters;
(3) Illumination— the solution comes;
(4) Verification— the idea is proved sound.

THAT WARMING-UP PERIOD

Back in the sixties, Hiram Everest was experimenting in his back yard with crude petroleum. After the lighter distillates came off, there remained a heavy dark residue which interested Everest, for he wondered to what commercial use it might be put. This interest was enlarging his knowledge to the point where he would presently emerge with the first marketable petroleum-base lubricants.

Back in the eighties, Dr. J. S. Pemberton was puttering about a kettle in an Atlanta kitchen. At a nearby drug store was one of the only three soda fountains in the city. Over and over a series of experiments would result in another brown syrup. As fast as one syrup was completed, Dr. Pemberton would rush to the soda fountain and test a drink made by charging the syrup with carbonated water. That was the "warming-up" period for Coca-Cola.

Also, in the nineties, Charles William Post arrived in Battle Creek. His money was gone, his physical well-being also. While he lay in the sun hoping for normal health to return, he realized that many others were also ailing, and he mulled over the question of how he might help them as well as himself. In other words, Post was "warming up" for his two inventions— Postum and Grape-Nuts.

One day a clothing salesman was complaining about the lack of opportunity for advancement in his field. I do not know much about clothing, but I asked him whether he had ever read any books on woolens and whether he followed the clothing trade journals or the magazines on salesmanship. He had never made use of this printed material although directly across from his store was one of the finest libraries in the country.

Probably no one ever made more elaborate preparation for his creative thinking than Charles Goodyear, who sought a method of vulcanizing rubber. In a rare old book which he wrote many years ago, he prophesied many fanciful uses for rubber. He even predicted rubber furniture, and a hard rubber table which he made in those early days still stands in the offices of one of the big rubber companies. Some of his predictions were realized. One who asked where to find him in those early days was thus advised: "Go to Staten Island. When you meet a man in a rubber coat, with rubber boots, a rubber cap and a rubber purse without a cent in it, you will find that he is Charles Goodyear." This "warming-up" process is not restricted to certain conditions or surroundings. Creative thinking simply involves interested investigation in every direction; this should supply the soil, seed, and fertilizer for a crop of new ideas.

INTO THE FIRELESS COOKER

Robert R. Updegraff has given a graphic description of what happens next. He speaks of the ingredients thus gathered as being placed raw into the fireless cooker; nothing seems to be happening but cooking proceeds just the same. Yes; unconscious creation may go on even in dreams or on the golf course. The only thing that may seriously interrupt the process is a switch to some other problem so utterly absorbing that the previous one is expelled from the mind entirely; however, that is almost impossible. Sometimes, even, we put hash into the fireless cooker and bring out a porterhouse steak, just as Henry Ford did with his 50-cent watch and as Perkins did when he sought synthetic quinine and got an aniline dye.

Sometimes we think that the problem is baffling only to find that after we have dismissed it entirely from mind— for days, weeks, perhaps years — the solution appears most unexpectedly. Many good ideas have arrived long after the thinker gave up hope.

There is more than one way to use this mental fireless cooker. After talking with many original thinkers— business men, engineers, inventors, writers, artists, and others — it seems to me that this Incubation period is best assisted by consulting our own personal inclination as to what we should do. In gathering material for preparation, our line of action is fairly well defined.

But in the next step we are, in a sense, seeking distraction from the problem. We want to lie fallow or, to change the figure of speech, we seek to rest on our oars for a time and ride along on momentum.

The most effective distraction is indulgence in that form of lessened activity which appeals most to our personal likes. This advice seems fairly well proved, for creative men and women report that they get their best ideas in different ways— one while walking, another while on a train ride, another at the theater, a fourth in the garden. Note that the ideas come usually while they are doing something they like to do. I cannot imagine nor have I ever heard of a man getting a brilliant idea while engaged in something for which he had a distinct distaste. Here a personal experience may help to illustrate my point.

Four men were working on the problem of marketing a novel product in a difficult new field. Much material was needed for preparation. To save time they broke their investigation into four sections, each man taking one. After gathering their facts and impressions they met to share their findings; then they scattered for a few days' thinking.

Man One locked himself in his office, refused all telephone calls, and wrote down suggestions all day long.

Man Two took a friend down on Long Island. Here the two swam and fished a great deal and discussed the problem at irregular intervals.

Man Three stepped into his car and drove rather aimlessly about Connecticut and Vermont. He says that he merely looked at people and merchants and considered in a loose way what might influence them to buy the goods he wanted to sell.

Man Four went home and alternated work in his garden with thought about the problem.

It would simplify matters to report that one of these methods showed better results than the others. But actually all four came back with equally good ideas.

Mere sleep may be all that is required for successful "fireless cooking." That is why thinkers through all time have liked to steep themselves in a problem before going to bed.

Many incidents might be related in which problems have been solved in dreams. A simpler use of this possibility that ideas may come with relaxation is offered by the use of couches in two New York offices. When the executives must get new ideas on short notice, their practice is to charge their minds with the problem during the morning, eat little lunch and flop down on the couch for a half hour or more. They try their best to sleep or make their minds blank. They say it works, and since Huxley says, "Science is that which works," it must be scientific. There is some evidence to show that many of us do our best thinking when in a horizontal position.

One business executive believes that the use of two different offices helps him to get new ideas. His factory is in a small town outside of a big city. There he spends his mornings in the manufacturing atmosphere. At noon he motors to the city and goes to his other office which is also a local branch and showroom: here centers the local selling. This method of alternating factory and selling activity is a sound one in freshening thought. Also it gives him two fireless cookers— the factory is his fireless cooker for selling ideas, the sales office is his fireless cooker for manufacturing ideas. "Morning for creation, afternoon for routine work" is the rule which one advertising organization tries to maintain. Any executives who have creative work to do are not to be interrupted in the morning except in emergencies.

GETTING THE FLASH

An interesting story is told about the naming of Ivory Soap. The infant firm of Procter & Gamble wanted to make a soap of pure vegetable oils resembling castile. They bought a formula, made up a batch, and the soap turned out white. For a while they called it merely "White Soap," but they realized that some more distinctive name should be used. They talked the matter over without reaching a satisfactory decision. One Sunday morning at church, Harley Procter got his flash of inspiration. The Bible reading included the eighth verse of the forty-fifth Psalm: "All thy garments smell of myrrh, and aloes, and cassia, out of the ivory palaces, whereby they have made thee glad." "There," thought Procter, "is our name!" The members of the firm met again and agreed that the name "Ivory" should be given their soap.

Robert H. Ingersoll and his brother Charles built a small specialty business in New York. One day the elder brother saw a small clock in an office. He knew that its works were inexpensive compared to those of a watch, because they were made by machine instead of by hand. The "flash" told him that by making clockworks still smaller they could be fitted into a watchcase. This watch through mass production could be sold for far less than any timepiece then on the market. He tried to get a clockmaker to work on the problem but was told the feat would be impossible. So Ingersoll went ahead on his own and by 1893 the first Ingersoll Watch was offered to the public.

HOW CAN YOU PROVE IT WILL PAY?

In the realm of pure science we can afford to seek knowledge for its own sake; new discoveries that advance the borders of our knowledge are welcomed without reference to their commercial value. But in business every new idea must pay its way. How can we know it will? Not by relying entirely on our own judgment, nor by accepting the opinions of friends and business associates. If you make women's dresses, your girl employees may tell you that your new designs are beautiful, just to flatter you.

The practice of pretesting new designs and policies is on the increase, for we realize, after watching the failure of many innovations, that it is cheaper to test a sample than rush to large-scale operation and find that we were mistaken. So the new advertising idea is tested in many different ways before much money is spent on it. The novel selling policy can be tried in a few cities experimentally before making the decision to spread it over the nation. The new product can be shown to typical customers, in groups or singly, taking into account varying tastes of different parts of the country.

Even a young man writing to twenty hardware dealers for a position may well send his first letter to five merchants before deciding that it is worth mailing to all twenty. The owner of a roadside stand, when inventing a new dish which he and his friends think will appeal to hungry tourists, does well to offer samples to his regular customers before placing it permanently on the menu.

The full technique of testing is a big subject in itself; too big to cover here. In another book, The Sales Expansion Question Book, I have gathered over six hundred questions which have been found useful and suggestive in checking the value of new ideas in merchandise, packaging, selling, advertising, and other elements which make for success. The importance of face-to-face contact with those who sell and buy the goods cannot be overestimated. It is significant that many businesses which enjoy lasting vitality were started by men who dealt with their customers at first hand and thus learned from direct contact what people like or dislike. Thus the business was proved at every point, daily, from the outset, and the testing went on continuously through the period of development.

Whelan had a new idea about cigar stores and tested its soundness as a clerk in his own United Cigar Store.

Woolworth thought that a shop specializing in items to sell at five and ten cents would pay well. He kept his own store, and after two or three failures developed his idea to the point of profit.

Penney had an original idea about small town department stores and worked it out in his own proving ground— the first Penney Store.

Hartford thought that tea should be sold at lower prices and proved that it could be done profitably in the first of the A & P Stores.

Mennen sold his talcum in his own drug store and got the kicks and bouquets direct from his customers.

Waterman sold his own fountain pens behind a newsstand in New York, and if the customer got ink all over his fingers, the inventor knew that something had to be done about it.

If you are unwilling to test your new ideas, get some unbiased outsider to do it for you. Fortunes can be lost in the wrong kind of new ideas. And even an outstanding new idea usually emerges from the gauntlet in an improved form which increases its possibilities as a moneymaker.

INSIGHTS TO IMAGINATION:

Work to develop your own unique technique for going after new ideas. See what works best for you when it comes to alternating business and pleasure. Focusing completely on the challenge in front of you will most likely result in frustration.

Know that the warming up period can vary greatly depending on a number of factors. The warming up period for this book turned out to be three years. What is amazing is that during the three years, innovation and imagination have risen to the forefront of thought in business once again.

Read and re-read the last paragraph of this chapter. Look forward to testing. You will come out of the process with a better product or service than what you started with.

45 | making conditions work with you

chapter six

A RADIO BROADCASTER SAID RECENTLY THAT GEORGE M. Cohan writes most of his plays at night in a Times Square hotel. Others go off to the mountains to put their ideas into shape. A well-known writer of college textbooks admits privately that he prepared one of his best volumes in a room he hired in Chinatown; he felt that he would do better if he was entirely away from his usual environment. Working methods are always interesting. In the cases of writers, musicians, and artists, we find often that the imagination is stimulated in odd ways, but no one seems to have gathered similar material about business men.

Some find that their minds work best during or just after a walk. You will remember what Helmholtz said about the happy appearance of new ideas following "the slow ascent of wooded hills." John Cowper Powys writes, "Nietzsche maintained the admirable opinion that all exciting and enlarging human thoughts come to their originators' heads in the process of walking." Jastrow writes, "Thinkers have at all times resorted to the restful inspiration of a walk in the woods or a stroll over hill and dale." But some find their best thoughts while reclining, and E. E. Jones reports that Rossini, Milton, Leibniz, and Descartes belong to this brotherhood of those who think best while in a horizontal position.

Dr. Donald A. Laird believes that a certain amount of distraction forces us to concentrate and exert ourselves more vigorously, provided, of course, that the noise or bustle does not exceed certain limits. However, sustained mental effort is difficult in a boiler factory or with riveting going on next door. Thomas Carlyle could not stand even the crow of a cock, and built himself a soundproof room for thinking. Joseph Pulitzer and Mark Twain regarded noise as a positive menace to health as well as to effective thinking. Edison blessed his deafness as a real aid to concentration. Herbert Spencer put plugs in his ears to escape the distraction of nearby noises.

IT PAYS TO EXPERIMENT

Advocates may be found for all sorts of working methods and conditions ranging from those which are methodical and conventional to others which are disorderly and bizarre. This indicates that one should experiment to discover the methods and conditions which best fit in with his individual makeup.

Looking about, we will find that the most original minds in business are rarely clamped every minute to a desk; nor are they immersed in too much routine. From time to time every person should get away from his business, just as the painter has to step back from his canvas now and then for best results. M. L. Wilson, whose skill in advertising and selling showed in Interwoven Socks and Djer-Kiss Perfume, says that the greatest service he ever rendered one of his clients was to induce him to leave the office one day a week and play golf. Up to this point the manufacturer had done well, but he was taking the responsibility for every department of the business, and as the business grew his office became a madhouse where one person after another rushed in to consult him about routine trivialities. He had no time left for creative thinking. Wilson knew that this executive had to escape his squirrel cage if he were to refresh his mind and allow his best thoughts to rise to the surface. This belief was vindicated by results; one day a week away from the office, even when that day was devoted solely to recreation, brought new ideas that doubled the business in a few years' time.

WATCH THE THERMOMETER
AS WELL AS THE CLOCK

In *Increasing Personal Efficiency*, Donald Laird gives some physiological hints to those who want to improve their thinking. He finds that most people work best at a temperature of 65° F. This efficiency drops when the thermometer falls below 48° or rises above 68°. However, we all know exceptional people who think best with their coats and vests on during the hottest August days, and we have met human polar bears who like their offices icy cold. But if we are average human beings, Laird's findings suggests that a swim in a Y. M. C. A. pool during lunch hour may be helpful to mental efficiency during dog days, while wetting the head and wrists with cold water may serve the same purpose.

Laird offers evidence that for most of us efficiency rises to two peaks a year— in April and again in October. This observation falls in with general experience. Expansive ideas come most naturally in spring and fall. If we can arrange our work so that our most active thinking period coincides with this rise in efficiency, we enlist another ally in our battle for new ideas. Part of the stimulation of April and October is due to the variable weather conditions of these months. Mental efficiency is greater in countries where the climate varies than in those countries where it runs along on an even level. So here is another tip: we can sometimes create weather variation by opening the window wider or altering the adjustment on the office radiator. Fresh air drills and calisthenics can help in an office as well as in a school.

While humidity lowers mental efficiency, so does dried out air in a steam-heated room, and in winter means should be used to keep the atmosphere moist.

In general, mental efficiency is at its peak in the morning and declines steadily as the day goes forward. There is a slight rise again

47

after the evening meal. So we may as well watch the clock after all, and work with it. One business executive found out the value of a flying start in a rather unusual way. He moved from the city to a suburban village fifty minutes away. Something unpleasant happened; he noticed after a few months that he was duller in the morning than when he had lived in the city. He wondered why. He felt that his living conditions were improved by the change with more outdoor recreation, better air, and sounder sleep. Finally he came to this conclusion: The difference in his morning trip was responsible. To use his own words: "When I lived in the city, I reached my office in only twenty minutes. I traveled to work among strangers. I had time for only a superficial examination of the newspaper. No absorbing or relaxing conditions distracted me; my mind was set on the day's work and nothing else, and so I plunged into it without any need to work up steam.

"Out in the suburbs, my morning start was entirely different. I had many train acquaintances, usually sat beside one of them, and we visited most of the way in. Often I played bridge in the smoking car. If I sat alone, I usually found something absorbing to read in the newspaper and got definitely interested in topics unrelated to my day's work. As a result, my morning energy— that alertness and freshness which is greatest early in the day— was dulled by the time I sat down to work. I enjoyed these social contacts on the morning train ride, but I was forced to conclude that they were luxuries which I could not afford. Now I devote the morning ride to something that keeps or sharpens this freshness. I may do work on papers which I carry in my brief case, or I read trade papers or business books. Call me a 'crab' if you like— and I suppose some do— I will not, if I can help it, sit beside some friend or acquaintance in the morning; it is too expensive! On making this change, the old freshness came back again. I'm glad to ride with friends or play bridge in the train on the way home in the evening— that's different. It's relaxing and pleasant. I want to relax in the evening, but not in the morning." This experience is a reminder that our social life or seemingly harmless conditions may serve as a direct drag or accelerant to our effectiveness at thinking.

We have seen that the creative thinker usually has wide interests. To follow these he must use much of his spare time. He cannot be monopolized by friends or even his own family. He is in touch with many people rather than a constant runner with the herd or the same little group, and this spread of interests is essential to his continued ability to think creatively. To many, he is confusing. Some misunderstand him entirely and think he is aloof. The development and constructive use of his imagination depends on many contacts, varying stimuli, freedom from too much routine after the day's work. He is not like the artist who works independently all day long; the business man has routine affairs which occupy much or nearly all of his day. To add routine social life to the business routine is to cut down on his chances of being original. Some of us are so busy with irrelevant, nonproductive and trivial routine that we haven't even time for a hobby.

HOW TO SPEND A LUNCH HOUR

While I first began to write advertisements, I sat in an open office with three grand fellows. We thoroughly enjoyed each other's company. The best proof was that we went out regularly together for lunch. We were with a new company and our fellowship served a good purpose in welding us to each other and building old-fashioned "house pride." But our worth to ourselves and to our employers depended on our originality. After a few weeks, the day-after-day sameness of our lunch hour began to pall on us. Perhaps we were just a little ashamed to admit this, but shortly we broke up and scattered off to lunch in pairs or singly to seek outsiders, indulging in our foursome only once a week or so.

Some day I hope to expound more fully a philosophy of how to spend the lunch hour. There is not room enough here to do this subject justice, but I would like to summarize a few of the points I have in mind.

Let us begin by assuming that you work hard during the morning. We assume also that you want to work at full capacity throughout the afternoon.

It simply is not sound practice to work also during lunch hour, for this may cut down your afternoon efficiency to an extent that more than cancels any progress made during noon hour. It is not practical either to go in a perfunctory way to the same eating place in the same old way and eat pretty much the same old lunch.

Lunch time is the golden recess of the working day, your chance to get your second wind, to recuperate from your morning's expenditure of energy, to refresh yourself by diverting your mind as much as possible. It may be the rest period when the morning's thinking is put into the fireless cooker to stew away for afternoon results.

The way in which you spend lunch hour determines to a large extent the value you get out of your afternoon. Make it as distracting a change as you can. If you have been grinding at some problem in the solitude of your private office, telephone your most diverting friend to go to lunch with you, and take a brisk walk if possible. If you have conferred all morning with heavy-minded associates, take Florence, the telephone operator, out to lunch, if you don't mind being seen with her in public. Or maybe you're so talked out that you need the pleasure of your own exclusive company in some unpopular restaurant where most of the tables stand empty.

Don't eat the same way every day. Take chances on new eating places and new dishes. You've been preached to about eating light. The chief value of the light lunch has never been advertised: it is that a quick sandwich leaves time for a walk. Go to some unfamiliar part of town, visit some unfamiliar department in a nearby department store, browse around in a book store, sit down in a convenient park, step inside an open church. That last advice was given me by a salesman who spends at least one noon hour a week in a church, and he says that it is the greatest freshener he knows, for it gets him furthest away from his business atmosphere

GIVE THE HORSE HER HEAD

Cromwell once made a remark that will sound irrational to many who read these pages. He said, "He goes further who knows not whither he is going." "Napoleon," writes Dr. Hirsch, "believed that battles were won as a result of abrupt inspiration on the field of battle—the emotional excitement serving merely as an inspiration inaugurating condition for the victorious intuition, the latter being grounded on previous acquired knowledge and high mental ability." In other words, Napoleon did not always know whither he was going.

The value of a fixed objective is obvious, but it is possible to have such set ideas about a goal that we fail to see an even larger possibility as we travel toward our original objective. Pantasote entered the market as a chair covering but later enjoyed a much larger volume of business as topping for automobiles. Bull Durham was born a pipe tobacco, but greater tonnage was sold when "Bull" was discovered to be good makings for cigarettes. The nonskid automobile tire was designed originally as a specialty to be sold in sandy country; later it became the prevailing type everywhere.

Walter Drey, who has developed a most original and successful plan of selling typewriters to youngsters, tells me that by letting his plans shift and change as he went along they grew bigger and better than he had ever expected. Others feel the same way. Small companies often outwit and outmaneuver large ones just because the big company more commonly has more settled routine and tightly planned objectives. That makes the big company slower to put new plans into operation. We can't afford to lose flexibility!

PLAY AND ORIGINALITY

In some respects, flexibility is close kin to the play impulse. In his report on the educational exhibit at Venice, Sequin says: "The nations which had the most toys had, too, more individuality, ideality, and heroism. The nations which have been made famous by their artists, artisans, and idealists, supplied their infants with toys."

In "make believe" children get new ideas and new combinations. A characteristic of child's play is the shifting from one thing to another; interest is allowed to change as fancy dictates. This changing from one thing to another promotes mental growth and originality. That was why Darwin delighted in "fool's experiments." Again, the play of the child alternates between fantasy or daydreaming and objective action; the fishing pole is seen as the knight's lance and then handled as though it really were one. Fanciful thinking of this kind often leads to new ideas. Robert S. Woodworth advises us to "Give invention free rein for the time being, and come around with criticism later." This is the practice of one successful acquaintance of mine. He says: "Bring me the wildest ideas you can think up. The more unusual they are, the better I will like them. I can tone a wild idea down and make it practical, but I can never blow the breath of life into an idea that is little and mediocre."

Stepping into A. W. Diller's office one day I saw beside his desk a blank white card, covered with picture glass, and nicely framed. Diller was using this as a focus point for fresh ideas just as Kant used to stare at a distant tower. Another business thinker had a jeweler engrave on a circular disc of silver a figure representing the annual sales volume he wanted to build. He carried this pocket piece as a constant reminder of his objective. He believes that it does not pay to think too much about the separate steps between you and your goal; if you have the objective strongly enough in mind the steps take care of themselves. At times this seems true enough. It is like connecting two points with a straight line; so long as you keep looking at the point from which your pencil starts you have difficulty. But the minute you look at the point which is your destination you find that the pencil travels in a straight line toward it and almost without effort.

IDEAS ON SCHEDULE

Some get new ideas through faith in their ability to live up to a self-imposed schedule. They say to clients, "I will have a new selling plan ready for you by March 12th," or "I will come in on

Thursday at four o'clock with a new package design." This working method mobilizes all one's resources on the rush. Or you may decide not to move from the spot until you have the needed new idea. In Advertising of Selling, we read Gerard Lambert's account of the creation of the halitosis theme for Listerine advertising. He says: "Seagrove and Feasley arrived in St. Louis and I took them into my brother Marion's office with him and closed the door and told them that we were going to come out of the room with an idea for Listerine. We debated all the possibilities and suddenly dear old Marion suggested 'bad breath.' We all jumped on him for such an indecent thought. Once more he brought it up and again it was outlawed by us. The third time I yelled over the low partition to Mr. Deacon and asked him to come in.

"When he came in I asked him if Listerine was any good for bad breath. He said, 'Wait a moment,' and produced a tremendous scrapbook from medical journals and opened it on his lap. I stood looking over his shoulder and as he recited one headline, saying that Listerine was good for halitosis, I stopped him and said, 'What is that?' 'Why, Gerard,' he said, 'that is the medical term for unpleasant breath.' I said, 'Wait a minute, say that again.' Feasley spoke up and said, 'There is something we can hang our hat on.' We kicked the old gentleman out of the room totally unaware of what had happened and the four of us immediately began to spark on the idea."

53

INSIGHTS TO IMAGINATION:

What time of day do you do your best work? Where do you find yourself most productive? Are there certain activities that stimulate your creative thought most freely?

Don't worry if you don't have the answers yet. Spend some time over the next few days observing yourself. The answers will come to you.

Giles mentions the benefits of the morning commute. Our technology makes it even easier than ever to truly derive benefit from this time of the day. Instead of wondering which self-help CD program you should bring with you, you can load them all onto an MP3 player. Whatever technology you use the key question is: Is your commute preparing you for the day or sapping your creative energy?

The same could be asked of your lunch hour. Look at the ways Giles suggests spending a lunch hour. Try something different and enjoy the new results you get.

55 | the sex urge and the body-mind reserves

chapter seven

NATHANIEL D. MTTRON HIRSCH, IN A BOOK called Genius and Creative Intelligence, writes, "The creative process of genius also arises forth from a psycho-physiological state in which there is a surplus of energy." He then describes some of the circumstances which help build up this Body-Mind Reserve. Generally speaking, the creative thinker, consciously or unconsciously, seeks to avoid time wastes and energy leakages which are all too common with most of us. The genius avoids complicated social adjustments. Often he dodges family life and its many responsibilities. "From the lesser functioning of the acquisitive, gregarious, self-assertive, self-submissive, parental, and sex instincts, a reserve of psycho-physiological energy is accumulated which is drawn upon in the creative period," writes Hirsch.

On first thought, this need of a Body-Mind Reserve suggests that creative thinking can go hand in hand only with a superior body, and we ask, then how about Carlyle, Emerson, Darwin, Disraeli, Dickens, John Burroughs, and hundreds of others who have had ill health? How about the odd little discovery by Ellis that geniuses are five times as subject to gout as are others? George Jean Nathan has even gone so far as to say, "Art is the child of ill-health."

The point is rather that, if our health is substandard and our surplus low, we should husband what energy we have if we want to do creative work. This may demand that we work intensively during fewer hours of the day, as did Darwin and others. The routine part of our work we should handle carefully but mechanically, not trying to mix imagination with routine. Rather, we should lay aside problems demanding imagination for some definite but convenient period when we can give them undivided attention.

We might take a tip from Vash Young. At lunch one day, some weeks before Vash brought out his second book, Let's Start Over Again, he told me of his plan to kill off worry, or at least to reduce its crucifying load. If you read his book, you will remember that Vash does not tell you to cut out worry— no, indeed! He advises you to worry all you like, but be sure that you make a really good job of it. When you find yourself worrying throughout the day, stop short before the worry monopolizes you and lay it aside in the ice box until next day. Select one hour out of every twenty-four as a Worry Hour. Then gather together all your worries, and give them your concentrated attention when the proper time comes. Perhaps you will decide to spend the hour from eight to nine each morning in worrying; thus you will do justice to your worrying, you will be more efficient at your day's work, and if you finally decide that you want to worry less, you can cut the hour in half or even less. I have wandered from the point, but it was worth while. Perhaps Vash Young's scheme will help you to worry less. That helps in building up your BodyMind Reserve for creative thinking. Worry is imagination gone wild on a destructive spree. By reversal you can convert the same energy into imagination used for more constructive purposes.

Why not a Constructive Imagination Hour, selected to fit in every day's program wherever it can to best advantage? During the day, while you wait on table or play an adding machine or lay bricks, interesting ideas may come to you. But the routine and mechanics of your job demand your attention; there is no time to stop and think. Very well; make a mental note of each idea. Better still, jot it down on a pad for consideration during your Imagination Hour. One hour a day spent in constructive imagination will soon lead to one of two results: either it will uncover ability which you did not realize you had—or you will find that you are hopelessly stupid. The odds are all against this second possibility. Honestly!

Returning to our chapter theme: that phrase "Psycho-Physiological Reserve" brought to a head some odds and ends that appeared in my notes on creative thinking. I think it was Spencer who said that we owe it to ourselves first of all to be vigorously healthy animals. If we have poor health, we owe it to ourselves and others to work out our program so that even with this handicap we have a Body-Mind Reserve on which we can draw.

We experience days when everything in the Body-Mind machine of ours functions vigorously and in unity, but these days are all too rare. We would like them to occur oftener. Sometimes these happy days come seemingly without reason, sometimes they are with us when the outlook is actually black and discouraging, while on still other days we feel happy but this creative urge may be entirely missing.

ALL ABOUT SEX

About two months before this book got under way; I was eating one noon with three men who are quite original in their chosen fields. We were talking about hobbies. Every two or three years I write a book; I had this one in mind at the time and outlined some of the things I thought should go into it.

"You ought to have a chapter on sex," said one of our quartet, and he expressed the idea that perhaps some sort of extramarital arrangement helped creative thinking, particularly for the tired business man. "There's nothing to that," declared a second of the group, a man of fifty-five, whose imagination has distinguished him in three different kinds of business. "The least productive year

I ever had was one when I had a mistress. The best year I ever spent was one in which I was a total abstainer so far as sex relationships were concerned. Both of these years occurred in my thirties."

"My own idea," ventured the third, who is rather a hardboiled, unsentimental sort of person, "is that you can fall in love with other things besides women. What's more, you can get quite as much kick out of it." He went on to say that he had a fine brown wench of a cello that he had just taken to his heart, and he added that from this new love he got all the enlivening and expansive stimulation that came with the love affair that culminated in his happy marriage. He isn't out of love with his wife a bit; but he has added a cello as a mistress, and he says he really thinks of the relationship in that way. "I have discovered that my new love for music carries over fresh energy into every department of my life, particularly the creative side," he concluded. Perhaps Emerson wrote from a similar viewpoint when he said, "... a man's library is a sort of harem." Such is the variety of experience you run into when you get people to open wide on the subject of sex.

Since this is no textbook, and since the author is far from being an authority on sex, perhaps the few facts following may help to throw some light on the relation between sexual matters and creative thinking.

In a magazine article, "Sex Madness," that genial authority, Dr. Logan Clendening, writes: "I believe that a rigid code of conduct in sexual matters will make better men and women...men and women who have the personal qualities that we value— loyalty, dependableness, restraint, courage, urbanity, unselfishness, and companionship. And those who are loose in their sexual ethics are likely to possess all those qualities which make acquaintance with people a personal tragedy—shiftiness, lightness, selfishness, callousness, coarseness, jealousy, and lack of faith. The richness and glory of life are due to its devotions and not to its treasons."

That does not sound as though Clendening thinks a Body-Mind Reserve is hampered by the marriage customs we have built up. As a matter of fact, he believes that they grow out of the best experience of ages. So much has been printed on the other side that we might consider here some facts which indicate that perhaps sex is not the whole thing after all.

CHASTE ARTISTS

Hirsch says that sex relationships have been overstressed in the lives of geniuses, and that mental giants often put the whole sex business out of their minds for longer periods than do ordinary people. They may indulge in irregularities and make up for lost time after the painting is done, or the opera composed, but during the creative period they are not taking chances with that precious Body-Mind Reserve. Traveling salesmen, elevator boys, and tired business executives take note!

Havelock Ellis reports that about 10 percent of the real geniuses he studied never married, while an abnormally large percentage are sterile. Ordinarily we classify artists as the loosest, sexiest lot of all. Well, how would you like to paint like Corot? Or model and paint like Michelangelo?

Thomas Craven, one of our foremost art critics, gives us this information about these creative giants:

"Corot never married and never, so far as I know, had any sexual experience, preserving throughout his life his naive belief in the purity and divinity of all women.... Physically, however, he was as robustly constituted as Turner, rising before dawn to observe the morning twilight, a ceaseless worker, producing some 2,500 canvases, and like Turner again, covering most of Western Europe in his travels."

Michelangelo "took no pleasure in eating or drinking, or in carnal recreations."

A doctor whose practice is mostly among business and professional men in the higher-income brackets says, "Thank heaven if you are unhappily married for it can be one of the best stimulants to personal ambition and inventiveness that I know of."

Well, we four at the lunch table talked some more about sex

and its bearing on creative thinking. And the one man at the table who has an engineering mind and prefers the broad aspects of a subject rather than details, remarked: "So far as I am concerned, I am not interested in a few sex experiences or experiments here and there. You can prove anything you want to about sex. Marie Stopes, the lady writer, turns out a book that is a best seller on the subject and her views in some important respects are quite contrary to those of Van de Velde who is a specialist on the subject and is so recognized in medical circles. On top of that, both are Europeans and fail to take into consideration certain very different conditions in America.

"Why not look only at the obvious facts and the results of mass experimentation over the years? For centuries, the Oriental has made more of sex activity and sex technic than the European or the American. We are a frigid, abstemious lot compared to the Chinese, the Japs, the Turks, the Hindus, and the Arabs. Does it cramp our ability to think? Has it threatened our ability to invent, paint, write novels, compose music?

"Among the natives of Africa, and the South Seas, sex comes into life early, goes along furiously and with the utmost freedom and candor. No silly inhibitions there! But how about the mental creativeness of the natives?

"So far as our own Caucasian stock goes, I don't see that creative thinking is more successful among groups and in countries where marriage comes earlier or where sex irregularities are accepted as part of life. Rather the contrary. Nor does art or music flare up brightest among the loosest groups in our own country any more than we get the best business ideas or scientific discoveries from gigolos."

At which point we called for the check, matched for it, and scattered.

To this might be added three short paragraphs.

One. Clendening says "... sex is forever likely to be an individual matter."

Two. The widespread featuring of sexual irregularities in novels and on the stage should not make us feel that something is missing if we fall below the standards of Casanova or Catherine the Great.

Three. However you work it out for yourself, remember the Body-Mind Reserve; if you want to trap new ideas you'll need it.

FISH, CHOCOLATE AND EYE EXERCISES

At forty, runs an old proverb, a man is either a fool or his own best physician. One artist saves his haircuts for times when he feels mentally stale. No doctor told him that barber's shears and combs refresh tired brains— he found it out for himself. It helps to restore his Body-Mind Reserve. So does a shampoo; baths, too-quick hot ones, long neutral ones. And osteopath's fingers. Often some surprisingly simple measure helps wonderfully to restore flagging energy.

Dr. Berman quotes Gerard to the effect that the Spartans ate watercress with their bread to increase wisdom. Only a few weeks before I read this, a friend of mine had a biochemist tell him to eat watercress every day because it contains some chemical which is good for brains. Liebig wrote, "There can be no thinking without phosphorus," and people rushed to eat fish. Many have been brought up to think of fish as brain food and so it is, but many qualifications should go with the statement, and they are too technical to put down here. How about the Eskimo? He lives almost entirely on sea food. Why doesn't all that phosphorus and iodine make him the most original man on earth?

We used to think that Body-Mind Reserve demanded a standard "balanced" diet, but now it is becoming apparent that no two persons thrive best on the same kinds of foods. Does a craving for a certain food mean that we should eat it plentifully? Perhaps, but an aversion to certain foods is usually a more reliable guide. A biochemist who is frequently consulted on obscure physical disorders performs seeming miracles by getting one person to eat more tomatoes while another regains the sparkle in his eyes by mixing the juices of celery, watercress and parsley and drinking a wineglassful before his evening meal. But biochemistry is a complicated subject and even the well-posted physician cannot always tell you just how to fit it in with your personal needs.

Gandhi believes that the quality of his thinking depends largely on what goes into his stomach, and he has experimented elaborately to learn what foods help establish the mental attitude he desires.

When they are exhausted but have to go right on thinking just the same, several business friends of mine have different ways of whipping up the Body-Mind Reserve.

One opens a desk drawer, pulls out a box of chocolates and eats five or six. That is stimulating. Sugar supplies energy quickly. Raw cocoa, from which chocolate is made, contains 2 percent theobromine, an alkaloid which is less stimulating but more nutritious than the alkaloid of tea or coffee. Chocolate helps soldiers on the march and it stimulates thinking, too, by restoring energy.

Others drink Coca-Cola or coffee. The English practice of drinking tea at four in the afternoon is a sound one. I have met with it in only one American business office, but it was interesting to discover that the enterprise depended on a steady flow of sound creative thinking. Tests show that coffee improves accuracy at the typewriter, and even a producer of decaffeinized coffee pays mixed respects to coffee in its natural state. In a Kaffee Hag Coffee booklet we read, "Caffeine stimulates thought and the association of ideas, thus producing wakefulness and sometimes mental confusion."

Another executive drinks freely of baking soda and water when he feels lethargic. He declares that his own states of stupidity often arise from acidosis. When he recovers his alkalinity, he finds the Body-Mind Reserve ample.

Much Body-Mind fatigue comes through the eyes. Too often we use them at short range all day long and any oculist will tell you that eyes were not designed to be used that way. Kant indulged in a sound physiological practice when he looked up now and then from his work and out at a distant tower. The change of focus was restful to his eyes and to his whole nervous system. Those who sit near windows where they can look at some distant view or object should try imitating Kant. If you still feel tired in the head, try rolling your eyes in the widest circle you can while the lids are closed. Swing eyes sideways from right to left, then back again, over and over, feeling a distinct pull. One man says he conserves mental energy enormously by shutting his eyes whenever he rides from one business call to another in subway, trolley or taxi.

THINKING, FAST AND SLOW

Mental concentration may be followed by physical tension. One friend takes special walks after dark— "special," because he loosens himself all he can and walks like a drunken man, so long as no one is looking. To the staggering gait he adds plenty of shoulder and arm stretching. This can be done in your home or back yard, if your family is sympathetic. When you get tension out of the body, you will usually find that it has evaporated also from the mind.

Around four o'clock in the afternoon, the clerks in a big department store leave their counters for a brief visit to the washroom. They are ordered to go at that time and splash their faces with cold water. The store management has learned that the Body-Mind Reserve becomes less as the day goes on and the salespeople tend to be tense and irritable. Whatever creative thinking they have left runs to the invention of new cutting remarks for exasperating customers. Washing the face in cold water refreshes the clerk in such a way that complaints from customers have been reduced by half.

Some minds are too speedy; others too sluggish. One business executive whose thyroid is not exactly right complained that his thoughts raced so rapidly that before he could throw salt on the tail of one idea, another had come to crowd it out. A gland specialist gave him a prescription which tamed him down. Now he can grasp an idea when it comes within range and hold on long enough to develop it. More common, no doubt, is the sluggish mind that finds difficulty in getting up momentum. Quicker physical action may help—a brisk walk at noon, a game of handball, a few minutes at boxing. One psychologist advises people of this sluggish type to quicken their physical actions—walk faster, rise from their chairs more briskly, gesticulate freely and vigorously, and, in short, speed up in every body movement. Since the Body-Mind machine is a unit, whatever stimulates the body helps the mind at the same time.

On roofs of buildings in larger cities you will find, at noon, business men enjoying sun baths, playing handball, tossing medicine balls. In one of the newer hotels, business people swim at noon in a pool flooded with ultraviolet rays. Sunshine is relaxing and refreshing. As indicated in the previous chapter, lunch time offers a golden opportunity to make afternoon thinking more efficient if you can only find out the something that thoroughly refreshes you in the time available.

If smoking seems to help your thinking, don't read that discouraging book, *How To Live*, authorized by the Hygiene Reference Board of the Life Extension Institute, Inc. Here Fisher and Fisk admit that "Nicotine causes brief stimulation of brain and spinal cord," but they add that this result is "followed by depression." They add: "The stimulating effect on the brain is so brief that tobacco can not properly be termed a stimulant. Its effect is narcotic and deadening. Those who fancy their thoughts flow more readily under the use of tobacco are in the same class with any other habitué whose thoughts can not flow serenely except under his accustomed indulgence. That a sound, healthy man, who has never been accustomed to the use of tobacco, can do better mental or physical work with tobacco than without it has never been shown." And the authors supply several tables of facts in verification of this dismal finding.

Alcohol slows one down and interferes with memory. You may feel ever so much brighter but you are only fooling yourself.

Some time try putting down all those clever ideas that come to you from keg or bottle and see how they look the next day. However, other authorities admit that alcohol, like certain toxins, may paralyze inhibitions and thus free creative powers lying dormant in the subconscious.

Read all the health books you like, but don't forget that your Body-Mind experimental station is different from all others, and you must be more or less a law unto yourself. The best diet, living condition, and surroundings are the ones which build up your own Body-Mind Reserve.

INSIGHTS TO IMAGINATION:

How can you add a Constructive Imagination Hour to your day? One of the keys is to capture your thoughts and ideas on paper so you can review them later during your hour.

What a great story Giles writes about the department store at 4 o'clock. Imagine something so easy and effective. Can you do something similar for yourself or the people who work for you? What a wonderful way to reduce customer complaints by half.

As Giles mentions, we each have a unique way to build our body-mind reserve. Do you know what your ideal reserve is?

67 | how the wide swing improves your thinking

WILLIAM H. WOODIN, SECRETARY OF THE UNITED STATES Treasury, music lover, composer, and outstanding business executive, writes in Etude: "Music study with a good teacher is one of the most sensible investments a parent can provide for a child— not with the view to making him a professional musician, but with the idea of giving him the wonderful mental acceleration that music brings, the great energizing force of the art, and the soul-cleansing qualities which only beautiful music seems to have.

"These effects of music remain a mystery, even to its most devout investigators. It is difficult for me, for instance, to understand how it is possible to play through a piece and at the same time have one's mind upon an entirely different subject. The mind is doing two distinctly different things at once. This has happened to me many, many times; and I have noted the very peculiar phenomenon that a problem, which had seemed baffling before a period of devotion to music, has by some peculiar process become clarified almost to the point of solution, after the period with music. Of course, it is a common experience to have problems, that seemed insolvable at the end of the day, work out splendidly after a night of sleep. Music seems to have a similar inexplicable effect of a more definite type. I do not know the psychology of this; I am only reciting things confirmed by my personal experience."

Mr. Woodin lists as other music lovers who are prominent in public life, Lord Balfour of England, Premier Mussolini of Italy, former Premier Edouard Herriot of France, Premier Painleve, former Vice President Dawes, former Speaker Longworth, Albert Einstein, Charles M. Schwab, Dr. Charles Mayo, and, looking at the past, Thomas Jefferson and Benjamin Franklin.

But Woodin's experience with his hobby contains a suggestion. His work as Secretary of the Treasury and as president of the American Car and Foundry Company offers a sharp contrast to his spare-time interest in musical composition. In his mental life extremes meet. This seems one key to using spare time as a feeder to creative ability.

> By letting our mental interests swing violently from one subject or mood to its opposite we widen our range and improve our changes of being inventive.

Recall Professor Whitehead's statement, "It is no paradox to say that in our most theoretical moods we may be nearest to our most practical applications." Doubtless Whitehead was referring to the theoretical mood which may suggest, for example, a radically new means of power production, followed by the creation of a new power plant, whose practicability and utility are then demonstrated through tests. The creative thinker in business who wants to scale the heights should be both a fanciful theorist and a hardboiled tester. His mind must be capable of dreaming air castles and then converting them into stone ones.

Woodin's success in business indicates that he is capable of making these wide swings from theory to practice. In choosing music as his hobby he makes another wide swing, for the creation of music is as far removed from the creation of financial policies and iron castings as can well be imagined. When we return to Woodin's list of other prominent men whose hobby is music, we find that they, too, make wide swings. Not one is a poet or an artist; Mussolini dynamic political thinker; Einstein-creative thinker in physics; Dawes— another creative thinker in the field of finance; Schwab-hard-headed steel salesman; Mayo-creative surgeon.

It looks as though a hobby, to be the best feeder to creative ability, should lie at the opposite pole from one's daily work.

Because: Two interests are better than one and the wider the separation is between those interests, the greater one's mental range.

And because: A spare-time interest which is utterly absorbing and unlike the day's work tends to crowd out conscious thought about daily problems. Thus we give the unconscious a chance to work on those problems requiring our best originality of thought. No one who looks deeply into this subject will doubt that a business executive may easily be originating a new sales policy in his unconscious at the very time when the human eye says that he is painting a still life! Woodin's experience bears this out: "The mind is doing two distinctly different things at once ... a problem, which had seemed baffling before a period of devotion to music, has by some peculiar process become clarified almost to the point of solution, after the period with music."

WORKS BOTH WAYS

It is a good rule that works both ways. How about musicians? Does a wide swing help them in solving problems of musical composition?

Haydn once said, "When my work does not advance, I retire into the oratory with my rosary and say an *Ave*; immediately ideas come to me."

Mozart, while playing billiards, created the beautiful music of the quintet in *The Magic Flute*.

William James once remarked that one of his friends when bothered by a problem deliberately thought of something quite different, and always with good results.

Someone has said that little improvements in a business come from within while the big ones come from outside. This value of the wide swing is proved further by the success enjoyed by many business executives transplanted from one field to another with which they may be quite unacquainted. Why should a department store executive be so successful when transplanted to a steel mill? How do we explain the success of a typewriter salesman made president of a bank? Or a history professor turned advertising agent?

Since most of us are confined rather closely to a particular kind of work during the week, it is obvious that the handling of our spare time determines to some extent our progress in developing creative imagination.

In the choice of hobbies, instinct may guide us rightly. A Coolidge or a Hoover, constantly pursued by visitors, committees, and politicians, goes off to fish over the weekend. Here the quiet and freedom to ponder one's own ideas provides a sharp contrast to the week's work of listening to others.

The Prince of Wales knits scarfs in his spare time. A nice, quiet, solitary interest, that a wide swing away from the bustling, incessant contacts he must make as heir apparent to the thrones of Great Britain and India. Several friends with wide circles of business acquaintances agree with me that the freshest minds seem to indulge in wide swings. Henry Clay Folger, a famous Standard Oil executive, became in his spare time an expert on the life and works of Shakespeare. But let us consider a hypothetical case—an imaginary comparison between two bank cashiers.

Cashier One makes coin collecting his hobby.

Cashier Two plays in an amateur band.

Undoubtedly Cashier One gets new light on his business from coin collecting. Coin collecting seems like a natural feeder for a bank cashier. But handling and inspecting old coins is too closely related to handling and inspecting new currency. A bank cashier's hobby ought to get him out among people in groups, should have some physical activity in it, and would be still better if carried on in the fresh air.

Cashier Two's hobby has none of the shortcomings of coin collecting. Playing in a band provides him with a much wider swing-group contacts of a social nature together with indoor and outdoor physical activity. The chances are that he returns from his hobby to the cashier's cage fresher and brighter than Cashier One.

So, if your business is confining, highly intellectual, involving endless conferences and consultations, you might in your spare time try breeding horses or raising cabbages.

If you own a woman's specialty shop, you may want an extra dose of masculine companionship at night.

If you run a book store, perhaps you should take up bowling.

If you sit all day at a mail-order business selling to stamp collectors—dancing and deer hunting with a group of friends may be just what you need out of working hours.

The wide swing bears on other problems than that of choosing one's hobby; there are other benefits one may get from making wide swings. The middle ground in life may be more comfortable, but it is the swing from one extreme to another that gives us greater mental stimulation.

The Swing from Likenesses to Differences. If you own a drug store, it will pay you to alternate a study of other successful drug stores with study of retail outlets in entirely different lines. Perhaps you will find more usable new ideas for your drug store from a study of filling stations or millinery stores than you can get from your fellow druggists.

The Swing from the Ideal to the Real. This book has emphasized the importance of understanding people as they really are. But it does no harm now and then to idealize people and think of what they ought to have or might be made to want in spite of their present characteristics or preferences.

The Swing from One's Admirers to One's Critics. Since the average individual tends to either overrate or underestimate his ability, it is well to alternate contacts with our admirers and our critics. The faith of our admirers is stimulating and builds confidence. From the comments of our critics we learn to keep our feet on the ground.

The Swing from Radicalism to Conservatism. You should know the changes impending in your industry or vocation. If you sell shoes, what radical experiments are being tested in the designing, manufacturing, and retailing of footwear? Which of these novel ideas promise to become the standard practices of tomorrow? Even if the new idea is a foolish one you ought to be familiar with it. It may suggest to you a still different idea, one which will be revolutionary. After contemplation of radical ideas, it pays to swing back to conservative practices and look again at them in a fresh light. You may find yourself tempted to throw away old practices simply because of their age; perhaps your consideration of the new will now suggest some improvement in an old practice or product.

The Swing from our Superiors to our Inferiors. Through association with the masters in our industry or profession we are stimulated to raise our own performance to a higher level. Through association with our inferiors we gain confidence and the realization that, though we have a long way to go, there are others who have not yet caught up to us.

The Swing from Similar to Dissimilar Associates. Wordsworth, Southey, Coleridge, and De Quincey met and stimulated each other; Emerson, Thoreau, Hawthorne, and Alcott did the same. Why are most of the automobile manufacturers in or near Detroit? Why is Paris the home of nearly all the couturiers? Why do so many of the best flute players come from Belgium? and the organists from England? Why must tires come from Akron and gloves from Gloversville? Is there such a thing as a mental contagion? Can we do our best among others who are aiming at similar goals? Perhaps, but we should mix also with people quite unlike us both in temperament and in vocation. We need our Rotary Clubs as well as our trade associations if we are to balance our specialized knowledge with the broadening effect of diversified contacts.

The Swing from Classes to Masses. If we make or sell a product or service of interest to people in different income classes, we may be confused by the separate problems of influencing each group. One rather simple solution to this problem is to make special studies of the two extremes of our consuming market—swinging from the rich intellectual to the poor illiterate. If we understand the two extremes, we will not have much trouble with the middle groups.

The basic importance of wide swings is that life itself is nothing but a series of wide swings—the swing from day to night, from companionship to solitude, from love to hate, from war to peace, from health to disease, from optimism to fear, from radicalism to conservatism, from prosperity to depression and from heat to cold. We are always on the way up or on the way down; few of us stay long in the middle ground.

If you talk with both your satisfied and your dissatisfied customers, you will have a far better idea of your problems and how to solve them than if you examine only the bouquets that are thrown your way. Many of us linger too long among "averages" where thinking may be dull and heavy. The original thinker in business has a more colorful imagination because his mind swings in a wider range than does that of the average man.

73

INSIGHTS TO IMAGINATION:

Do you have a hobby? After reviewing this chapter, is your hobby similar to your work or at the opposite end of the spectrum?

Are you listening to your critics? Very often the criticism will contain a germ of an idea that could launch your business in a

whole new direction. At the very least it's an opportunity to improve a possible deficiency.

However you do it, make it a habit to practice the wide swing
with your mind.

| what emotions stimulate creative thought?

chapter nine

I N 1851, GAIL BORDEN WAS SAILING HOME FROM England. At a World Fair in London, he had been awarded a medal for two concentrated foods invented to meet the needs of prospectors who joined the gold rush to California. Now, as he walked the decks, Borden was struck by a greater need in ocean travel.

Eighty years ago there was but one way to provide fresh milk for transatlantic travelers. Cows were brought aboard ship along with the passengers, for no refrigeration existed to keep milk from souring. On this voyage the milk supply was so inadequate that several babies became sick.

Borden's sympathy was stirred, and this time an even greater invention was to come from him than the two which earned the medal in London. He saw the need of supplying milk in a form which could be easily stored and protected against spoilage or contamination. One day as he watched a steaming tea kettle, it occurred to him that much of the water might be evaporated from cow's milk and that the condensed remainder might be sealed in cans where it would keep indefinitely. Such milk would be useful not only on the sea, but on land as well where fresh milk was difficult to obtain. Five years later Gail Borden was awarded a patent for "producing concentrated milk by evaporation in vacuo... the same having no sugar or other foreign matter mixed with it." Pity had created a new product having large commercial possibilities.

Devotion to his mother, and the desire to free her from the necessity of running a boarding house, was one of the emotional stimulants which spurred George Eastman into perfecting photography for the amateur.

Amadeo P. Giannini retired from active business at the age of thirty-one, with money enough to provide for his simple wants. One day he decided that he did not like the way in which banks were run. This dissatisfaction led to the opening of his own bank where he found greater success and a wider field than he had dreamed of in his previous work.

George Westinghouse, while riding on a train one day, became so irritated over the inefficiency of its brakes that he resolved to find a way to stop trains without jerks. His invention of the air brake was hastened by an emotional state approaching anger.

Dunlop wanted to ease the declining years of his mother whose poor health compelled her to sit in a wheel chair. The wheels had metal rims. Seeking to cushion her chair against the inequalities of the floor, he replaced the metal rims with rubber. From this affectionate impulse the first automobile tire came as a byproduct.

Dr. T. B. Welch felt strongly that "unfermented wine" was Scriptural and that it should be used in communion service instead of fermented wine. His experiments resulted in Welch Grape Juice, a commercial business of large proportions.

Alexander Graham Bell fell in love with a deaf girl. After she became his wife, he tried to devise an electrical device by which she might hear. From his experiments came principles of acoustics which made the telephone possible.

One manufacturer of my acquaintance was harassed by the labor union. It was not enough that he met all of their wage demands, nor that his factory was cleaner and lighter than those of competitors. His willingness to comply with every other requirement the labor men could think of was of no avail in maintaining harmony. Agitation from outside kept his men in a state of unrest.

At that time his goods were made entirely by hand. Mechanical production had been thought of but most manufacturers had the fixed idea that merchandise of this sort could not be made to equal existing standards. Finally, the unrest in this factory so angered the executives that they opened a little experimental plant some three hundred miles away. This secret factory was dedicated to the task of finding a way to make the goods by machinery. After two years that goal was reached, and the new goods were even more uniform than those made by hand. Better still, they could be sold at lower prices. All this came because the management had been stirred to a fighting pitch and this emotional stimulus spurred them into doing what had been considered impossible.

Robert Louis Stevenson makes one of his characters in St. Ives declare, "There is no telling what a man can do until he is thoroughly frightened." In creative thinking this might be altered to read, "There is no telling what a man can do until he falls in love, or is stirred by the desire to be great, or is thoroughly disgusted with something, or becomes angry at obstacles, or gets a lust for money, or finds himself face to face with poverty, or is otherwise stimulated by some emotion which works him up to concert pitch of inventiveness."

DR. CANNON'S EXPLANATION

Dr. Walter B. Cannon has written a famous book called *Bodily Changes in Pain, Hunger, Fear and Rage*. While it deals with the effects of emotions on the body, it is equally true that emotions may have the same quickening and energizing effects on the mind. In many emotional states one's energy is redirected, blood shifts to new seats of action, including the central nervous system. "I had to think fast," a salesman or manufacturer often says in describing some situation which was so emotionally stimulating that he was surprised at the fertility of thought which accompanied it. Dr.

Cannon finds that these states are "directly serviceable in making the organism more effective in the violent display of energy."

Darwin believed that some men unconsciously work themselves into a state of anger for the purpose of self-reinvigoration. Physical feats ordinarily impossible become easy when one is stirred by these emotions, while activity of thought is also accelerated. After commenting on the effects of emotional disturbances, Dr. Cannon goes on to say: "In this connection it is highly significant that in times of strong excitement there is not infrequent testimony to a sense of overwhelming power that sweeps in like a sudden tide and lifts the person to a new high level of ability. A friend of mine, whose nature is somewhat choleric, has told me that when he is seized with anger, he is also possessed by an intense conviction that he could crush and utterly destroy the object of his hostility. And I have heard a football player confess that just before the final game such an access of strength seemed to come to him that he felt able, on the signal, to crouch and with a jump go crashing through any ordinary door. There is intense satisfaction in these moments of supreme elation, when the body is at the acme of its accomplishment. And it is altogether probable that the critical dangers of adventure have a fascination because fear is thrilling, and extrication from a predicament, by calling forth all bodily resources and setting them to meet the challenge of the difficulty, yields many of the joys of conquest. For these reasons vigorous men go forth to seek dangers and to run large chances of serious injury. 'Danger makes us more alive. We so love to strive that we come to love the fear that gives us strength for conflict. Fear is not only something to be escaped from to a place of safety, but welcomed as an arsenal of augmented strength.' (Quoted from Hall.) And thus in the hazardous sports, in mountain climbing, in the hunting of big game, and in the tremendous adventure of war, risks and excitement and the sense of power surge up together, setting free unsuspected energies, and bringing vividly to consciousness memorable fresh revelations of the possibilities of achievement."

At this point the reader may be thinking, "Yes; but often I have been so emotionally upset that I couldn't see daylight at all, to say nothing of being able to think faster or better." We need to realize the fact that strong emotions may lead directly to more active, more creative thinking. Negative emotions may be transferred to positive ones. Fear should not paralyze us but be welcomed, as Dr. Cannon advises, for its value as an "arsenal of augmented strength."

Thus Gail Borden might have spent his pity in organizing a Society for the Prevention of Oceanic Travel by Babies. Fortunately, he found greater satisfaction in directing his emotion into a constructive solution of the problem which so aroused him.

George Westinghouse might have let his anger about the "damned inefficiency" of early brakes work itself off in a few caustic letters to newspapers about the backwardness of railroading. But the effort to invent better brakes provided a far better outlet for his energy and one that was decidedly profitable.

The stimulating value of positive emotions no one has ever doubted. Said Corot, "Never paint a subject unless it calls insistently and distinctly upon your eye and heart." When business problems are approached in this spirit, solutions often come which seem little short of inspirational. Whistler's most popular picture is his "Mother." Reproductions of this painting sell more extensively than do all of his other paintings and etchings combined. Recently "Mother" was brought from the Louvers to hang a few weeks in the Museum of Modern Art in New York. The occasion brought from art critics the reminder that Whistler said of this picture, "One does love to paint one's mummy nicely."

But emotional stimulation does more than speed the thought process. There is another side to this matter. We must consider well the emotions and instincts of those with whom we do business.

Every product we want to make or sell and every promising innovation of any kind should be weighed for its likelihood of appealing to some human emotion or desire. If no such possibility appears at first, thinking should be carried to the point of developing such an appeal. Creative imagination in business never overlooks the practical value of playing on the emotions.

Insights to Imagination:

Have you ever felt pity about a situation? Review the story of Gail Borden and how he turned his pity into a product that is still on grocery store shelves more than 150 years later.

Is there a product or service you feel could be done better? Is it something that interests you? Maybe you could stimulate your creative thought and do it better. There is always room for improvement. Why not you?

Review Giles interpretation of the Robert Louis Stevenson quote. There is tremendous power behind those words. Feel free to change man to woman.

Finally, what emotional desire will our innovation appeal to? The more desires it appeals to, the greater the likelihood of success.

81 | imagine yourself the customer

chapter ten

IMAGINE YOURSELF IN BUSINESS, MAKING BAND INSTRUMENTS. Two courses are open to you. One is to sell horns and drums by telling people why yours are good ones; there you stop. The other course is to set out deliberately to stir human desires which can be directly related to a bright new cornet or a big bass drum.

In the second approach, there is one thing which you most certainly will avoid; you will not attempt to sell your cornets merely as so much brass and workmanship. Nor will you be satisfied to describe only finishes, valves, mouthpieces, and so forth. You will enlist on your side every factor you can think of that will lead to the creation of more bands. You will do what you can to put new spirit into old bands, you will look into the possibility of creating bands where none now exist.

You will soon discover that to prospective owners of cornets the picture of playing in a band arouses more pleasurable images than you can possibly create by mere talk about the superiority of your cornet over others. And the more you can place these vivid images in the imagination of the possible customer, the more likely this interest is to reach the buying point. At all events that is what manufacturers of band instruments have discovered in their attempts to enlarge sales. So their sales promotion is aimed at a host of insistent desires, among which are these:

Desire to attract attention— he who plays a band instrument can hardly avoid doing that!

Desire to be great— the band marches at the head of the parade.

Desire to attract the opposite sex— girls are supposed to love bright uniforms and the glitter of brass.

Desire to be one of a select group— the band is nothing less.

Desire to be individual— your instrument may differ from the others, but if it doesn't, your playing at least is your personal self-expression.

Desire to make money— good players are often hired for parades, dances, and entertainments.

Desire for social success— as a player at dances and entertainments you meet new people.

Desire to be healthy— playing wind instruments is good for the lungs, and outdoor marching helps build you up.

Desire for a pleasant hobby— you get it in your music.

Desire to advance mentally— playing in the band helps you to appreciate music.

Desire to look one's best— most men do when in uniform.

Desire for play and amusement.

Desire for agreeable rivalry with one's fellows— there's a pleasant sort of competition for proficiency among the members of a band. Also, one band can compete with others.

Still other desires might be added to those listed here. My only object in going as far as I have is to emphasize the point that the more we can surround a product with pleasing images, the better our chances are of making sales. For simplicity no attempt is made here to distinguish between instincts, emotions, innate desires, impulses, and other psychological terms. Apparently there is no agreement among the psychologists themselves as to the exact definition of instinct. To the meticulous the listing of desires which follows will show duplication and overlapping, but better so than miss distinctions which may prove useful. Let us look at some common desires which the imaginative person always keeps in mind, either in designing merchandise or in selling it.

DESIRES— HOT AND COLD

The desire to be great is perhaps the leader of them all. When the Prince of Wales first wore blue shirts with attached collars, he started an epidemic which might never have been created by conventional sales promotion measures. When William Gillette played Sherlock Holmes and appeared on the stage in a dressing gown, the young men who saw him decided that they, too, would look distinguished in similar garments. When Irene Castle bobbed her hair, a wave of imitation followed like the wave of yawns that follows one hearty yawner in a street car. These incidents illustrate the prevalence of the desire to be great socially or through association with people more prominent than ourselves. They explain why testimonial advertising has been effective for years in stirring the desire to be great. Back in the early nineties, Russell Sage, the financier, permitted the makers of Allcock's Porous Plasters to publicize the fact that he preferred this means of curing a cold to any other. A perfumery company advertised Mrs. Grover Cleveland as a happy user. Advertisements for Waterman's Ideal Fountain Pen included endorsements from nearly everyone of prominence, including Chauncey Depew and Oliver Wendell Holmes. Testimonials from famous users were valuable in selling a public which had been disappointed in the shortcomings of two hundred other fountain pens.

Sound imagination faces the fact that in any attempt to revive an old business the start may best be made by getting bellwether customers whose patronage will influence those in a lower stratum of society. It is usually better to work from the top down.

In helping one of the three largest rubber companies, I ran into an interesting contrast between results where (1) you go first to the masses and (2) where you get the "better class" first and appeal to the masses later. During the World War the shortage of sole leather led this company to invent a compounded soling which had many good points. A subsidiary company was organized in England. In the United States the new sole was marketed after reasoning thus: "This composition sole wears better than leather. It is cheaper. Hence workingmen comprise the logical group to talk to at the start." Sales promotion was begun in this field and manufacturers of work shoes were quite responsive. But the sole has never been successful with other groups. And, from the start, even the workingmen seemed to look forward to the day when they could return to leather soles. This they did when the war ended and leather was again available.

In England, the story was a happier one. British shoe manufacturers discovered that the new sole was waterproof as well as durable. In that country it was sold first to makers of golf shoes. Here it served well. Better still, it won a sort of social standing at the very outset. Its merits impressed people of better-than-average purchasing power. From this start it was comparatively easy to interest manufacturers of street shoes and work shoes. Early sales were not notable, but by working from the top down large sales are enjoyed in Great Britain to this day, while sales in the United States have dropped to almost nothing.

A piano manufacturer finds that his most productive advertising is that done for used instruments autographed by famous opera stars. Yes; people like to shine by the reflected light of those more successful in life.

BANK VICE PRESIDENTS, ETC.

The multiplication of vice presidents in commerce and banking has come because the important customer's desire to be great can be catered to more effectively by putting him in touch with one having a title.

All of us want to be great financially. Hence, perhaps, the one headline in advertising which has won more readers than any other is the hackneyed old question, "Do you want to make more money?" Probably only one headline aimed at the yearning for financial greatness is more appealing, namely, "To men who want to recoup their losses during the next ten years." The itch to regain a lost joy or possession is always more insistent than the original desire of the same nature. Witness the effectiveness of appeals to women who want to remain attractive through the difficult forties. A hair tonic is sold more effectively through advertising to men whose hair is becoming thinner than by trying to sell it to young men as a dressing which improves their appearance. "Get back the old pep," is a potent appeal. Those who have lost their fortunes, their money, or their mental alertness may be fewer in number than those who are still on the upgrade, but their responsiveness is far greater when hope is aroused.

Desire to look one's best is also part of the desire to be great. I am advised that women choose their dresses for effect on their sisters, but my wife told me that, and I have my doubts. I know from experience that if I, as a man, want to look my best with other men, I dress rather differently than I would to draw favorable comments from women. Which suggests the *desire to attract the opposite sex*.

WHEN SEX APPEAL SOLD GASOLINE

It is several years since this experiment was made in a Brooklyn filling station. A company for which I wrote advertising reported that one of their dealers had increased sales rather handsomely by displacing his male attendants with pretty girls dressed in overalls. This one simple change made sales rise over 20 percent, if I remember rightly. (A natural question arises: If that is true, why aren't all filling station attendants women by this time? I can only reply that the results of valuable tests are often thrown away. Perhaps some puritanical director in the company saw the girls and made sarcastic comments to the president. Things like that do happen.)

This story, however, is quite believable when we look at another experiment made in a chain of phonograph stores, and tried at about the same time. Radio sets were just arriving to cut down the sales of phonographs and records. Little can be done to stay the passing of a dying industry; the most brilliant imagination cannot successfully raise the dead. However, the merchant I have in mind managed for a time to enlarge his business. About half of his clerks were men, while the other half were women. As a customer entered, any clerk who was idle stepped forward; that had been the practice. New instructions were issued: If the customer is a man, a woman clerk will wait on him; if the customer is a woman, a male clerk will take care of her. After the customer listened to the records he asked for, the salesperson was to suggest other discs. This dealer tells me that his customers seemed more willing to listen to and buy additional records when the suggestion came from one of the opposite sex.

GREGARIOUS, BUT—

Desire to be one of the Crowd. Desire to be an Individual. Most of us are gregarious— but not to the point of wanting to be exactly like our fellows. Many prefer to buy the most popular article of its kind, but even when Ford had no competition there was a huge sale of specialties made to add individuality to the old Model T. These specialties included special tops, oversize steering wheels, more efficient carburetors, non-fouling spark plugs, demountable rims. You could replace dozens of standard Ford parts with specialties.

When rouge came into more general use after the war, one color was satisfactory to most women. Soon it became apparent that rouge was needed in several shades to harmonize with various complexions. Women joined the growing number of rouge users only to follow up with demands for colors more expressive of their own individuality. Probably if there were one cigarette which tasted best to every smoker in the country many would still deprive themselves of "the best" for the sheer pleasure of being different, while many who were willing to follow the crowd would still strive to individualize themselves by owning novel cigarette cases, unusual cigarette lighters, and distinctive cigarette holders.

In some cases it pays to go clear over the line to benefit by a trait which McDougall calls "contra-imitation." "Contra-imitation" characterizes those who are completely emancipated and resist every inclination to join the crowd. They wear clothing made to their personal taste and measurements. Many years ago, an automobile manufacturer built both sales and prestige through advertising that he made only three cars a day. In 1932, another automobile builder whose sales fell drastically made the best of his predicament by advertising that during the year he would have only four hundred of his highest-priced cars to sell. Restricting output has been successful in many cases. If the article is one which has of necessity a limited sale, consider talk about exclusiveness. A good etching has high value partly because it is one of comparatively few impressions which the artist will approve as perfect. A book in a limited edition often sells quickly for the same reason. "Only three days more" has brought many a sale to a profitable close. Twenty-five copies of a Parisian frock may show better net profits than fifty.

AN EXPERIMENT THAT FAILED

He makes an article of men's wearing apparel. To describe it might reveal his identity, and I have no desire to do that. He was a poor second in his industry. The leader in this field set the pace in advertising and the trailers' advertising was a rather poor imitation. When the leader used certain kinds of pictures, the trailers followed. When the leader appeared with new advertising copy, the trailers imitated it to the best of their ability. I was asked to prepare some advertisements for the goods made by the second man in the field, and it seemed to me that he was simply playing into the enemy's hands. I agreed that the leader had the best possible advertising, but since he was spending about five times as much as any competitor, it did not seem that it was good strategy to follow his style of advertising too closely. I felt that it would be better to avoid similarity to the leader and so escape being a mere imitator in the minds of the public and merchants who carried the goods.

The leader's policy was to bring out one new model after another in rapid succession. He threw the whole weight of his advertising on each style as it arrived. In spite of this, dealers found it necessary to stock at least a dozen styles to satisfy all customers. The president agreed to test some advertising which reminded the consumer that the best style is that which suits the wearer's own personality, not some one general style worn by all. We went out to sell a line rather than one style at a time.

The advertising began. After a few months, sales showed an improvement, feeble at first but headed in the right direction. The public, at least in part, seemed to be catching the idea and agreeing with it. But that was not enough. The constant bang, bang, bang of the leader's costlier promotion was too much for the salesmen of my client. They could not free themselves from the idea that the leader could not possibly be wrong and that, therefore, we could not possibly be right. "Sure, we're getting more business, but we don't have so many calls for the latest models," they objected, proving that they had never caught the basic reason for our difference. The president stood by until he became victim of an influenza epidemic and had to stay at home for several months. He was away just long enough for his subordinates to outvote him and take up again with their imitative advertising. The business dwindled and about two years later the company was bought up by the leader.

This story is told here because it has a double significance. It sometimes pays to be contrary and not be hypnotized into running a business along certain lines just because the leader does it that way or because there are certain accepted customs in an industry. And the other point— an unpleasant one to record— is that even when originality succeeds there will still be those who deny its value.

INSIGHTS TO IMAGINATION:

Do you place VIVID images in the minds of your customers and potential customers? Do you know what images work best with your target audience?

Look at the list of desires in this chapter. How many of them do you incorporate?

Review the story of how sex appeal sold gasoline. One of the keys is that only one of the dealers tried the experiment. If you own or desire to own a business with numerous locations or sales-people, this lesson is critical. Is one of your locations or salespeople achieving remarkable success? If you can pinpoint the reasons for the success, then you can apply it to others in your company.

more about those insistent desires

chapter eleven

I N THE SEVENTEENTH CHAPTER OF THE ACTS, VERSES nineteen through twenty-one, we read: "And they took him, and brought him unto Areopagus, saying, May we know what this new doctrine, whereof thou speakest, is? For thou bringest certain strange things to our ears: we would know therefore what these things mean. *(For all the Athenians and strangers which were there spent their time in nothing else, but either to tell, or to hear some new thing)*". The italics are mine.

Apparently the Athenians and "the strangers" were as deeply interested in the new as we are today.

The *desire to appear progressive* is strong in many; their interest in the new never lets up. A New York department store has lately installed a shop which specializes in duplicates of frocks worn by stars in current moving picture hits. As we saw in our first chapter, advertising men for years have utilized in headlines the magic power of the word "New." And we like a peek at the future. Along with our love of the past steps our keen interest in what lies ahead. This interest has been appealed to in editorials by Arthur Brisbane, in novels by Jules Verne, in fantasies by Wells, and in stories, articles, and books by other popular writers.

The desire to put things together and take them apart is one that imagination frequently appeals to with handsome results. We see this interest actively appealed to in store window displays. One survey made of the average man's thoughts about shoes showed that the window display most commonly remembered was one which appeared about twenty years ago in Regal Shoe Stores. A buzz saw stood inside the window, sawing shoes in halves. This was showmanship which caught the imagination and, better still, indicated that Mr. Bliss was so confident that his shoes would prove better than others that he was glad to let the observer watch and compare.

At automobile shows the largest crowds usually gather around the stripped chasses. Even a lecturer, standing there, describing the features of the car in dry technical terms cannot drive the crowd away. A display of ingredients or raw materials or manufacturing processes rarely fails to attract a sizable crowd. Recently I was passing a men's clothing store in Boston. It had two windows. In one several suits were displayed— all attractive bargains, with prices well featured. In the other window a man was busily pushing some sort of scraping device over the floor and the window full of clothing stopped three observers. The window with the scraper was being watched by eighteen. The little cigar manufacturer who sits in his window inviting passers-by to watch his method of manufacture hitches up to this interest in construction. The rotisserie window gets extra attention by roasting its meats before the fire up front instead of burying its show in the kitchen. For a time, Lucky Strike Cigarettes won a Broadway audience by installing a midget factory in a corner store. Here Luckies were made for everyone to watch. Blackstone Cigars drew equally large crowds on the boardwalk in Atlantic City by showing how cigars were made by machinery.

LESS MISCHIEF FOR IDLE HANDS

One tool manufacturer found that he made better progress with amateur tool users when he published a clothbound book on how to work with tools and wood. It was written for the amateur tool user, and many thousands of copies were sold through hardware stores. Men and boys whose hobby was woodworking were also glad to buy plans which showed how to construct dog houses and ship models.

One store successfully sells a complete set of parts for an American Flag which modern Betsy Rosses can sew together. Unfinished furniture also appeals to the delight in using one's hands as well as to the desire for economy and individuality in one's furniture. Now knockdown furniture is coming in and its prospects are promising.

Sets of parts for ship models and stagecoaches are popular. As the favorite toy among boys, the Meccano type of construction set has replaced the lead soldier, and Marconi, beholding our boys at play, declared a while back that we are raising a nation of inventors.

Department stores stimulate their business by showing women how to plan dresses, make lamp shades, and paint china. One enterprising haberdasher placed a sign in his window announcing that he would gladly show customers how to tie bow ties with professional skill. A comparatively new hair tonic— Packer's Scalptone— appeals to this interest in construction. In the neck of the bottle is a vial of oil. If your scalp is dry, you mix all of this oil with the tonic. If your scalp is normal, you add only half the oil to the contents of the bottle. If you have an oily scalp, throw away the vial and use the tonic just as it comes to you.

One blue Monday, Sir Joshua Reynolds wrote, "There is no expedient to which a man will not resort to avoid the real labor of thinking." However, the *desire for mental power* has been successfully appealed to by many advertisers who offer the opportunity to master French in a few easy lessons, or learn "in a funny way" to play the piano. The Harvard Classics, memory courses, law courses, courses in becoming a railway mail clerk, short cuts to fame and conversational and commercial prowess—all appeal to this desire to progress.

The desire to overcome a bad habit may be capitalized too. For years Sherwin Cody has advertised to people who willingly pay money to some one who corrects their bad habit of saying, "He don't." In correct social manners are other shortcomings which many gladly pay to be rid of if a way is shown. In extending help to overcome a bad habit, your selling message should usually be coupled with a reminder of the freedom one thus secures to satisfy some other wish. The bad habit may interfere with social success or moneymaking ability or some other desirable condition, and so we remind the customer of positive benefits to come.

FROM PLAY TO PROTECTION

One of the most insistent desires is the *desire for play, amusement, participation in sports, relaxation, and laughter.* We took our World War seriously, and yet one type of speaker in Liberty Loan drives always did well. He was the talker who leavened his salesmanship with amusing comments and stories. Advertising with a touch of humor often gets better attention than do more solemn texts; many times the light touch outsells heavy, serious copy which appeared previously for the same article. One study of the attention value of advertisements of different sizes (conducted by Dr. Gallup and Carroll Rheinstrom) showed that a series of advertisements measuring only five inches in depth and a single column in width, got more attention from both men and women than the average full-page advertisement in the same weekly periodicals. Quarter pages with amusing sales approaches were remembered longer than conventional selling in much larger space. But does humor really sell goods? Yes, if it is tied up inseparably with good salesmanship. From my own experience I can recall humorous advertising prepared for high-priced luggage, chewing gum, confectionery, cigars, lubricating oil, and a few other commodities, all of which paid well. But the merit of the sales theme must always be put ahead of mere humor. Humor is justified only when it reinforces the sales message and makes it more emphatic.

The story of Sunny Jim, that humorous character which advertised Force, has been referred to many times in books and in articles and editorials on advertising as an example of the dangers of letting humor overshadow the product itself. I was a school-boy when Sunny Jim first appeared, but some years later F. J. Ross was invited to see what he could do to revive Force. He sent me out to call on grocers and consumers to discover what they actually knew about this breakfast food. Quickly it became evident that the main reason for buying Force had never been brought home to either the grocers or the public. To the simple question, "What is Force made of?" one grocer after another replied that he thought it was made of corn, while others did not know. One ruddy fellow told me, "Veil, I know dot it's a serious." Women were equally uncertain. Only a few knew the important fact that Force was made of wheat. Since wheat costs more than corn, Force was more expensive to make than corn flakes. Force had appeared as a pioneer flaked cereal all ready to eat without cooking. Later came the corn flakes. The corn flakes looked liked Force and the taste was not so different. The corn flake packages were bigger than the Force package. Sunny Jim advertised Force but he did not tell readers that it was a wheat cereal and hence worth more than corn flakes. Humor had been used primarily to get attention and goodwill rather than to emphasize a selling feature. That is one danger in humor, it is so attractive of itself that the user may be tempted to rely on it to the extent of weakening his salesmanship.

J. K. Fraser's well-remembered advertisements for Sapolio were strong because in "Spotless Town" every type of user discovered that one article after another could be made cleaner with Sapolio. "Spotless Town" was a strong selling idea above all; the humor was only a pleasant method of presentation.

There are other instances which prove the value of amusement and entertainment in business promotion. A few years before the Civil War, the first store was opened for what later became the Great Atlantic and Pacific Tea Company. Its location was on Vesey

Street in New York, and one record of those early days says that band concerts were held every Saturday night in the little tea shop which was later to expand into the only billion-dollar retailing chain. John Wanamaker's store gives free concerts for tired shoppers. Some day department stores may become even more popular by installing talking picture theaters for their customers.

More serious is the desire to protect one's possessions and dependents. This first suggests life insurance and investments, but the appeal may be tied to many cheaper commodities whose makers do not even realize that there is such a possibility.

In 1922, I was riding to work one morning beside a man who was a director on the boards of three large manufacturers. He was an unusual man who had proved himself more than normally inventive, having marketed several of his own patents. It was a warm day in early summer and the train windows were open. I was astonished to see him take from his pocket a small wad of toilet paper. Quite casually he peeled off a couple of sheets. Putting them to his nose he gave a hearty blow. Then he bunched the paper and threw it out the window. "I learned that trick when I was in Japan," he said, in a matter-of-fact way, and if I remember rightly, he also said that the Japanese use tissue paper for handkerchiefs. Inventor he may have been, but he did not see that this same idea in more refined form could be marketed successfully here in the United States. Some one else imagined that possibility later on, and turned his imagination into money. Today many who have colds use tissue paper handkerchiefs and throw them away– they have been interested by the protection it gives against the spread of germs.

Other appeals to this protective instinct are possible. More rugged tires are needed as protection against the dangers of blow-outs in today's fast driving. You are invited to protect your eyesight by using better light and more bulbs. You learn that decaffeinated coffee and denicotinized cigars will protect your heart. It is astonishing how many different products can be coupled with this desire to protect one's self and one's family or possessions. Where such a tie-up is justified, the appeal may be strong indeed.

Frank Rowe, an old friend and associate, put fresh emphasis on the worth of paint when somewhere in the middle of an advertisement he wrote "Save the Surface and You Save All." The protective value of paint had been advertised before, but Rowe presented that appeal in a more imaginative phrase which in turn appealed to the imagination of the reader with greater strength than could a ton of argumentative paint advertising. Among building supplies, roofing has captured the customers' imagination more successfully than most other materials used for home construction. Every home is a place of protection, but in many of the roofings that appeal has been compounded. Protection against fire and rotting are appeals which can be joined to roofing of asbestos, copper, zinc, and slate.

"PRIVATE"

The *desire for privacy or secrecy* is often used to promote sales.

Booklets on beauty treatments, reducing courses, and feminine hygiene may be requested by more women when offered in a "plain envelope" with no outside imprint to indicate the source of mailing. In the marketing of Kotex, it was found that sales in the drug store were helped by wrapping the box in plain paper, piling up the wrapped packages on the counter, and displaying a simple sign which stated the name and price. The bashful woman could thus avoid embarrassment by picking up a package and handing over her money without asking for Kotex by name.

Many take to home study more readily if the advertisement indicates that the courses can be carried on in private. Perhaps this is because the student has taken courses before, only to drop them before completion, and he is just a bit afraid of letting the family see him give in to this weakness again. Perhaps it is because he wants to keep the matter a secret until he is ready to astonish his wife, sweet-heart, or the "bunch" with his proficiency at the saxophone, on the dance floor, or in conversational Spanish.

"Body building" courses succeed in part because of the customer's anticipated delight in keeping his progress a secret until he exhibits those rippling new muscles next summer on the bathing beach.

The desire to get something for nothing is a trait which no psychologist talks about. But it always has been something to reckon with in business promotion. Many variations are possible: "this coupon is good for 10 cents," "three box tops are redeemable for a china cup," "Free Silver Spoon in every package." All premiums are aimed at this desire and so are "limited" offers, combination sales, "three packages for the price of two." Photographers come to your office and take your picture free of charge hoping that you will like the proofs well enough to order a dozen finished ones. Allowances on used goods help sales in many lines. A shoe store secured extra sales at a profit by making allowances on old shoes left by the customer. An alarm clock company did the same thing; so did a manufacturer of irons.

The desire to save time is a rich one to tap— particularly in these fast-moving days of pressing interests. It may be well to remind ourselves, however, that we want to save time only to spend it in satisfying some other desire. Hence those who most effectively capitalize this desire remind the listener of some pleasant way in which the time so saved may be employed. Less time spent in baking cookies leaves more time for bridge. The acquisition of culture on an expenditure of only fifteen minutes a day may be desirable to make way for pleasures of an earthier tang.

INSIGHTS TO IMAGINATION:

Look at all the desires Giles mentions. The tool manufacturer found two new ways to boost business: A How To Guide and plans for projects. These items lead to the purchase of more tools as the woodworker gets better and better. How could you incorporate this concept into what you do?

Think of how many extremely profitable businesses have been created to help people overcome bad habits. Is there a bad habit people want to break that your business can appeal to?

The story of how one man threw the potential for millions of dollars out of the train window was a reminder that we may have all done that at sometime. Or we have had an idea, done nothing, and seen the idea brought to market by someone else. That doesn't have to happen anymore.

99

101 | little loves that bring in money

chapter twelve

IN ADDITION TO THE DESIRES WHICH FILL THE TWO preceding chapters, imagination, if it is to be practical, must reckon with other loves that exist in most of us.

Love of Good Sportsmanship and Fair Play. The money-back offer came many years ago as a new method of winning back the confidence of those who had been cheated by sharp retailing practices and variable standards in merchandise. This willingness to refund purchase price where a customer is dissatisfied has been varied in many ways. Some ingenious appeals to this love of good sportsmanship are given by Richard Webster in Advertising & Selling. He writes:

"I. In the summer of 1931, 'I will bet anybody that DIAMOND is the finest GINGER ALE— Dan Leary,' was printed on bottle collars, on window streamers, and in Connecticut newspaper advertisement headlines: 20 cents is the price of a bottle. Dan Leary is General Manager of Diamond Ginger Ale Company, known throughout the state as a Democratic leader willing to back a winner.

"II. Conrad Razor Blades were introduced four in a package, with a single blade separately wrapped for trial. Refund of full amount on return of the 4-blade package in the original wrapper.

"III. Last August, when there was lots of loose talk about 'buying now before prices go up,' Magrane, Lynn department store, advertised that he would 'rebuy all unused sheets bought during this sale at any time from October 1 to November 1 at 10 cents each above prices paid during the sale.'

"IV. Sterling Products backs the effectiveness of consumer advertising by telling dealers: 'If the advertising does not quickly move from your shelves our standards, return them and you'll be given your money back.'

"V. Dealer advertising of Rockne Motor Cars last fall in place of copy generalizations on superior riding qualities, pledged $10 to anyone that tried a free demonstration ride in a Rockne Six and within a week purchased any other automobile in the same price class-under $600.

"VI. Bush Terminal, New York, makes a specific wager, 'YOUR RENT FREE for two years if you can't save what our estimate shows on manufacturing and distribution costs.' And, after actual examples of savings, the copy restates this posted wager: 'We guarantee our estimates: your rent is free for two years if you can't save what the estimate shows.'

"VII. George A. Hormel & Co., introducing Hormel Flavor Sealed Vegetable Soup, promised to pay back double the purchase price to anyone who doesn't think this product 'the best vegetable soup you ever bought.' In ten days 150,000 cans were sold in the Chicago trading area, and there were twelve requests for the refund.

"VIII. The current magazine advertising of Knox Gelatine promises to refund not merely the cost of the gelatine, but also of all other materials used in any dish which is not, in your judgment, far superior to what it was when you made it with any brand of flavored gelatine."

Love of Contrast. A little shoe store in 43rd Street, New York, got unusual attention for several weeks by displaying in its window a pair of the huge oxfords worn by Primo Carnera beside a pair of shoes worn by a circus midget. A lock salesman found that customers were far more interested in his sample case when he put several antique door fasteners inside and showed them before bringing out the modern locks he had for sale. Old and new-cheapest and most expensive-fat girl and living skeleton-tallest and shortest-all such contrasts, particularly when placed side by side, seem to have an appeal that is perennially strong.

Love of Motion. Moving displays arrest the eye more readily than do those which are static. The outdoor advertising companies had to stop one advertiser who attached to his billboards a device that flapped in the wind, for it killed off the attention paid to posters surrounding it.

It is our love of motion which draws us to automobiles, speed boats, bicycles, Kiddie Kars, chewing gum, yarn for knitting; in earlier days it sent our grandparents to the store for rocking chairs, chewing tobacco, and knives with which they whiled away time in whittling.

Love of Pets. One salesman found that he did better when he took his dog along with him, for many dealers wanted to talk dog with him, and this made more friendly relationships. A hardware dealer in Ohio had an interesting experience with pets. The family cat presented him with one of her periodical litters of kittens. He put them in the store window, but most of those who paused to look were little girls or old ladies, and neither of these feminine groups buy hardware. Later on this same hardware dealer borrowed four brother puppies and let them play about in the same window. This time he stopped more men and boys than women and girls, which was exactly what he wanted.

That pup which sits beside the furnace has made Bryant Heater advertising more effective. Those Scotch Terriers who sit alert and listening in Texaco advertising do double service by humanizing the page and by suggesting that Texaco Oil gives quieter engine performance. When advertising Keds sports shoes, Tom Young and I were thinking out a Prize Contest for boys and girls. We had only a limited amount of money, and we wanted to make it go as far as possible. Young suggested that wire-haired terriers be given as prizes. Without going into details, it was quickly proved that children thought a few hundred dollars' worth of dogs were much more attractive prizes than the same amount in cash. Another proof of the attention and memory value of a pet is supplied by the Victor fox terrier sitting in front of the phonograph, listening to "His master's voice." Not only did this trademark make Victor advertising long remembered; it served as a powerful suggestion that Victor tone was true to life. Cartoonists made this trademark the basis for cartoons, and editors adapted it to editorials.

Love of Controversy— including love of contests, games, and all activities where two sides are in opposition. Big league baseball gets along nicely without paid advertising; so great is public interest that the newspapers have to report all baseball activities as news.

Crusading or controversy in business may be either dangerous or quite profitable. One of the profitable crusades was that made on behalf of an advanced idea in automobile lubrication back in 1912. The Vacuum Oil Company made a motor oil called Mobiloil. Mobiloil came in several bodies, or degrees of heaviness, having somewhat different characteristics. This refiner's program of automobile lubrication was briefly that automobile engines of different makes had differing mechanical requirements which made it impossible for any one oil to lubricate all motors with scientific exactitude. Clearances between pistons and piston rings differed; so did the lubricating systems, temperature conditions, fits of main bearings. The Mobiloil plan to give a better fit in lubrication resembled in some ways the recent advertising of Knox Hats which calls attention to special models for long heads and round heads as well as the customary hats for heads of average shape.

At the time of which I am writing, other oil refiners produced only one lubricating oil for all engines— a light-bodied, light-colored lubricant. This practice was accepted generally and without much thought as to whether it was right or wrong. In its advertising to establish automobile lubrication on a more scientific basis, the first Mobiloil announcement carried the headline: "No one oil is best for all cars. *This is absolute.*" The text went on to explain why. It also explained that the Mobiloil Chart in some cases included special advice that certain cars use a different oil in winter than in summer. From the very start this controversial issue brought interesting results. Salesmen for other oil refiners applied for positions on the Mobiloil selling staff. This was one of the best indications that the advertising carried conviction. The Mobiloil salesmen had some of the feeling that they were fighters in a righteous cause, and here and there dealers caught the idea and sold with like conviction. In a few years' time this original idea made Mobiloil the leader in its field, and other oil refiners were revamping their businesses to refine oil in several grades also.

This interest in controversy is sometimes utilized in a distinctly aggressive way, as when George Washington Hill advertised, "Reach for a Lucky instead of a sweet," and coupled his advice with pictures of people grown pudgy from eating too much fattening food.

Love of Surprise or Novelty. A touch of the unexpected often stimulates sales where less imaginative handling fails. I knew one salesman who hung up a new record at selling canned salmon. When making his first call on a grocer he would ask first for the store cat. Next he would open a can of salmon and let her sniff. The cat would get excited at the smell of fish and make frantic efforts to reach the can. Then the salesman would say, "You can't fool a cat when it comes to that good fish smell!" Actually this demonstration proved little or nothing, but it was one of those trifles which swing orders. A good question to ask in considering a new idea is this: What little touch of the unexpected would make this appeal still more to the imagination?

105

Love of Noise. Few people can long endure absolute quiet; most people feel that the greater the noise the better the party. Oceans and brooks interest us as canals and ponds never can. "Love of noise" may seem to contradict the success of many devices which feature "quiet operation." But why do we want quiet automobiles? We wish to hear the sound of our own conversation. Perhaps this love of noise has limited application to business, but it is difficult to think of doing without the blast of the steamboat, the purr of the automobile, and the pop of a bottle of champagne. Some years ago Walker Evans put a telling statement in his advertising of a motor car equipped with a double jet carburetor. He characterized the engine as having a "sporting" and a "loafing" range. He called attention to the distinctly different sound when you drove fast. There was something special to listen to at high speed, a noise that distinguished the car. Vacuum cup tires were popular for some years because their sissing sound set them apart from other tires.

Love of Escape with its attendant thrill. Whether you peddle from door to door or are a physician trying to make a patient take her medicine, one strong way to influence your listener is to picture escape from a problem. Such a "thrill" with its escape from danger may seem weak compared with the thrill of speeding down a roller coaster, but they are blood cousins. If your new idea promises escape from some common problem, do not overlook this attraction in your selling. The Franklin car has earned a place through its ability to function perfectly in zero weather and without risk of freezing. Life insurance is attractive because it offers escape from the problem of protecting dependents in case of one's death. Retirement annuities are growing in popularity because they assure escape from the fear of being dependent on others when old age overtakes us.

Love of Gossip. A large company asked me to study its problems. One of many questions I asked was, "Is there any gossip in your field which may be operating against you?" The sales executive of whom I asked this grew quite excited. "Who told you to ask that?" he demanded as though there were a general plot against his company. "No one," I replied. "That is one of my stock questions, because it sometimes uncovers a real problem." It turned out that there was unfavorable trade gossip which was harmful to this manufacturer.

But the love of gossip may be turned to one's advantage. A leading oyster grower tells me that the best year he ever had was that when an unfounded rumor was circulated that oysters were on the road to extinction. People rushed to make the most of the oyster's last days. In another year an equally unfounded rumor went round that oysters were responsible for an epidemic of sickness, and sales fell off.

Love of One's Own— parents, kin, marriage partner, children, fellow lodge members, social group, fellow church members, etc. Advertising does well to glorify the user and his group. Walter H. Belcher built extra business on this love when he bought copies of Eddie Guest's book of "Mother" poems and enclosed one in each box of Lowney's Chocolates sold as a Mother's Day Special. An oil marketer made money by specializing on an engine lubricant for that select group which rides in Pierce Arrows.

Love of Brightness and Darkness in alternation— Early motorists liked bright red cars, but as time went on black were preferred. Then bright colors returned to popularity. This ebb and flow in color preference applies also to clothing and household furnishings. Women were glad to get brightly colored galoshes after wearing black rubbers for many years, but within a few seasons they turned again to dull colors.

Love of Comfort, Ease, Warmth, Indolence, and Freedom from responsibility. This gets close to—

Love of Pleasure through the Senses— which is worth a chapter by itself.

INSIGHTS TO IMAGINATION:

What do you love to do?

Review the eight examples Giles provides. Many of them are still being used today in advertising or sales promotion in one form or another. How could you best use one or more to promote your product or service?

Study the list of loves in this chapter. While not all of them may apply to your situation, pick out the two or three you feel will be most helpful. Use your imagination to see how to best apply them.

109 | stirring the senses with imagination

chapter thirteen

A WEALTHY NEW YORKER WHO OWNED SEVEN AUTOMOBILES could easily afford twenty more. Naturally he was the target for many salesmen. One of these had tried every approach he could think of, emphasized every mechanical advantage of his car, and advanced every argument he could muster. Nothing seemed to stir the slightest interest. Brown Landone tells how the youthful salesman came to him for advice. This was the suggestion: "You need to create desire... not by words, but by sense images.... Find out, if possible, to which one of the man's senses you should appeal. Can't you remember anything which will give us a clue?"

The salesman recalled one marked characteristic of the prospect; his fingers roved appraisingly over the surfaces of objects on his desk-the papers, the leather bindings of his books, the carvings of his Florentine desk set. He collected rare books, apparently because of the feel of their rich bindings. From this observation the salesman's imagination suggested an attempt to sell through the sense of touch. On his next call, the young man took with him an axle which had been cleaned and polished for special exhibition. Nothing could be smoother to the touch. The millionaire was asked to run his fingers over its hard, glossy surface, and as he did so his eyes sparkled, for never before had he felt anything so smooth. Then the salesman explained how this perfect finish of parts resulted not only in durability but in superlatively quiet operation. Inside of thirteen minutes, the millionaire ordered three automobiles.

The most vivid approach— the one surest to reach people of all types— is that aimed directly at their senses. Here is the one technique to which all respond, because it requires least thinking. Hence in using imagination to get a job, or create new products, new sales policies, new store personality, or more effective advertising, ask: "How can I strengthen the attraction of my new idea by hitching it directly to one or more of the five senses?"

MAKING SIGHT WORK FOR YOU

The furniture stock of the average store is a mere herding of tables, chairs, beds, and bureaus presented without imagination on the part of the merchant. When lined up as so many beds and tables this stock makes little appeal to the imagination of the customer. Acting on his business imagination, John Wanamaker added to his furniture department a "house palatial." He added later a completely furnished apartment and a home of more modest character. To the visual attractiveness of his furniture, he had plussed the still greater drawing power of furniture in actual home surroundings. The importance of reaching imagination through the eye can scarcely be overestimated. It has been proved that a colorful picture registers faster than can appeals to any other senses.

It is not enough that a product be well made; it must also look impressive or at least seem as good as any competitor. I was asked to help advertise a product selling to boys. It was the best of its kind, and so good were the materials that the article could be lighter and yet stronger than competitive goods. This lightness was an advantage, but it was found that boys were attracted still more to a competitive article which looked chunkier and sturdier. After several experiments I regretfully advised the manufacturer to give his goods a "beefier" appearance. The change added nothing to wear or service, but boys knew what they wanted and it was money wasted to try to educate them.

A luggage maker had a problem common in that field. In appearance his goods did not differ substantially from those which were cheaper. His superiority was hidden from the eye because it lay under the surface. After some study of competitive lines, I found that kits of parts and hidden materials were effective when used by the salesman to open new accounts. Similar kits in the hands of dealers enabled them in turn to show their customers just why it was worth a few dollars more to have a strongly attached handle, genuine cowhide and imported linings, and why one corner cap reinforced the whole trunk while another cap which superficially looked the same gave only a fraction as much protection.

Cigars wrapped in foil did not sell well because the customer could not see his purchase until he had bought and unwrapped it. The same cigar in cellophane was accepted immediately. Cellophane has helped many products because the customer gets wrapped and protected goods which he can see. Today, one canner is supplying grocers with sample tins having open tops covered with transparent material so that the housewife's eyes can tell her exactly what she is buying. Other manufacturers of products hidden heretofore in opaque containers now place inserts of cellophane in the sides of their boxes or cans so that the customer can do his window shopping before he buys.

A DeSoto advertisement contains a clever appeal to the eye. Beside the car on the showroom floor is a mirror, and as the prospective customer sits behind the wheel he sees himself as he will look when driving. No merchant needs to be told that attractive goods well exposed are half sold. He knows that his rent is determined largely by the number of people who pass his store daily, but few merchants realize how many dollars they can get from using a little imagination in their windows. Elmer J. Bliss, skillful merchant as well as successful manufacturer, has placed one striking picture after another in the windows of his Regal Shoe Stores. Mr. Bliss copied high-priced English shoes, stood them side by side with his Regal Reproductions, and defied those on the sidewalk to distinguish between originals and copies. Then he had a guessing contest with prizes for those who could tell the Regal shoe from the imported original.

One mistake in selling through the eye is common among manufacturers, merchants, and salesmen: they assume that mere visual presentation is enough when it should be considered only as a starting point. An electric toaster when given a window display sold rather poorly; when it was put instead on a table covered with a doily and accompanied by a complete breakfast setting including a plate of toast, sales rose 200 percent. In store windows, as in advertising, the product should often be shown in use rather than as a mere piece of merchandise.

When baby grand pianos were new, Lyon & Healey offered in magazine advertising a free paper pattern to be laid on the floor. This showed the exact dimensions of their baby grands, and as you placed the pattern on the rug you saw in your imagination a phantom image of the real piano rising from it.

In another book, *Breaking Through Competition*, I pointed to some of the considerations that attend the use of color in merchandising. In the case of a new 5-cent confection, two packages were suggested which were identical in design but one was red while the other was blue. These were shown to a few hundred men and women. Nearly all of the men chose the blue package while almost without exception the women chose red. Some time later I learned that in this country Jastrow made tests which indicate that, generally speaking, men prefer blue while red is the color quickest to attract women. In Europe, Wissler's test carried him to the same conclusion. This finding should not be accepted as applicable to every color problem, for while red seems to be the most acceptable color for a box of chocolates, it is true that expensive chocolates are bought by men as gifts to women. However, another indication of the soundness of this finding about red and blue is that blue shirts with attached collars are popular among men but pink shirts sell poorly.

Since we are seen before being heard in any attempt to get work or make sales, we should look well to the effect we make on the eyes. The rotisserie manager cooks his meats out in front where the picture wakens appetites of passers-by. The one-man cigar manufacturer rolls his tobacco in the front window to make you want a fresh cigar. The cobbler has his machinery up front to show you that his equipment is modern. A white vanilla dessert found that by changing to pink it could multiply previous sales by six.

"SMELLS"— PLUS AND MINUS

For years Lifebuoy Soap made little progress in this country for few liked its carbolated odor. Early advertising stressed the "clean smell" of the soap, but that was not very successful. Finally, a startling advertising shift was made to unpleasant body odor and the promise was made that Lifebuoy would take B.O. away. Then the rise in sales began in earnest. Listerine was only a modest tuckaway in drug stores until protection against halitosis was publicized.

Novel raincoats were unsaleable because of their rubbery odor. Two months later the same coats were selling on a big scale, all because the rubber had been given a totally different odor. Today special odors can be built into many products. In some cases the leather smell is being subtracted from animal hides; in others imitation leather goods are impregnated with the odor of the real thing. A deodorizing or perfuming process may turn a commercial wall-flower into a best seller. One automobile agent who is particularly successful in selling to women always sprays a mild perfume inside his sedans in the showroom. Other experiments with odor include perfumed hosiery and paints, scented ink and even coal with a pine odor which "Gives to your home a pleasant and healthful odor and also acts as a cold preventive."

Some smells even suggest efficiency. Many like a shampoo soap strong in tar. Glover's Mange Cure, originally planned for dogs, made its way to barber shops and home medicine cabinets because it smelled powerful enough to kill any dandruff germ. Sloan's Liniment, first prescribed for horses, appealed to human beings because it smelled efficient enough to penetrate aching joints and muscles. A seller of bacon is impregnating his wrapping paper with special bacon aroma to reinforce the natural appeal of the product. A Connecticut fire insurance company solicits business by means of circulars scented with the odor of wet burned wood which smells like the day after the conflagration. On the Pacific Coast a manufacturer now turns out garlic sauce which leaves no garlic breath.

Creative business imagination suggests that (1) you can reinforce natural fragrance, (2) you can deodorize unacceptable odors, and (3) you can replace objectionable odors with attractive ones.

LISTEN!

To a great extent, the six-cylinder automobile engine won its way on its superiority to the ear; it sounded so much smoother than a four. Then the eight came along with an even greater appeal to the ear. Recently Laurence G. Meads told me about a man who sells cars having twelve cylinders. The most important word in his selling talk is a lightly whispered "psssh." He says to the possible owner: "You come to the foot of the steepest hill and she goes up psssh! You accelerate to eighty miles an hour and all you hear is psssh! You stop in traffic and jump away at the green light, but you hear nothing but a little psssh!"

That is an example of real imagination in selling, imagination on the part of the salesman, imagination that appeals to the imagination of the listener— a beautiful appeal to the ears. On the other hand, there are times when noise may be a selling asset—the owner of a motorcycle would hardly enjoy himself if it rolled along in absolute silence; here noise means life and power! In some parts of the country and with certain types of consumers, dealers will tell you that a distinct squeak still helps to sell shoes. To most folks the hum of a vacuum cleaner suggests efficiency, and to a camera fan the rustle of a Graflex curtain in action suggests efficiency that can never be associated with the mere click of a between-the-lens shutter.

Years ago, Thomas Edison routed opera stars around the country to sing their arias in public while standing beside his phonograph. The vocalist would commence, break off, and the song would be completed by the phonograph. Supposedly you couldn't tell where the singer stopped and the phonograph began. Later on, the sales manager for another phonograph hid his instrument behind a curtain along with three makes of phonographs which were then more popular. The salesman stepped behind the curtain and played the same record on all four phonographs. It is claimed that most listeners chose the phonograph that subjected itself to this comparative test.

SAMPLING THE TASTE

"It's perfectly astonishing," says a buyer for a grocery store chain, "how often a salesman will attempt to sell taste through a word description when offering a sample would serve so much better." The salesmen for a beverage which may be quickly prepared carry a thermos flask of hot water and mix up samples on the spot. The salesmen for a sandwich spread buy loaves of bread from the grocers, bring out bread knives, open cans of their goods, and serve up sample sandwiches on the spot. Where preparation of a food takes more time, salesmen may send packages to dealers' homes so that their families can learn about it. The manufacturer of a new line of chocolates got distribution in record time through delivering generous samples at jobbers' homes. A small town druggist flavors the glue on his postage stamps so that when the buyer licks it he finds a more agreeable taste than is provided by Uncle Sam.

One problem which sometimes arises in appealing to taste is that of getting the customer to prefer the flavor of your goods to the taste of a competitive product which he has bought and used for a long time. A smoker may be induced to try your pipe tobacco, and it may be superior to what he has been using, but he doesn't like it on the first trial simply because it "tastes different." If you can get him to smoke your tobacco for several days in succession, he may not like his former brand when he returns to it, for his taste will now be "set" in your favor. Where this problem occurs, any sample should be ample for several trials of the product. Perhaps you will decide to sell a week's supply at a bargain price, just to get the new customer properly launched.

FEELS GOOD!

In studying the African-American market, I ran into two business experiences which offer an amusing light on the African American's sense of touch. One concerned cigars; a manufacturer said that his sales among the African Americans were better than average. He was cultivating this market while many of his competitors did not. Said he: "I even have a special shape for them. Just imagine yourself a big colored fellow. You don't like the feel of a cigarette or little cigar in those heavy lips of yours, but a big cigar feels swell."

A linoleum salesman took his line into the South. As he built up trade, he noticed that demand was abnormally large for his darker colors. When he did a little detective work, he discovered that the lighter shades contained a greater percent of certain pigments which made them feel chilly to the African American who walked barefoot about his house, while the darker linoleum contained more cork and so felt warmer against bare skin.

This serves as a useful reminder. The appeal to touch need not be confined to fingers. We feel with our feet-eyes, even with our shoes on. That is why hotels and exclusive stores lay thick velvety carpets. Even the feeling of chairs may influence sales; and a cooling system helps summer sales in stores. Sometimes only an emergency will stimulate imagination into doing justice to sense appeal. During a coal strike, sellers of electric heaters discovered a simple appeal to the desire for warmth and comfort. A platform truck carried a giant electric heater through the streets. The enlarged heater projected its growing warmth out to pedestrians twenty feet away. Merchants put heaters against their show windows and the warmth was transmitted through plate glass to people on the sidewalks. Still other retailers placed heating devices out in the open where the surrounding cold emphasized the fact that there are more ways to get warm than one.

INSIGHTS TO IMAGINATION:

Create. What a powerful word. How can you create desire? Use your imagination to create an appeal to the five senses.

Giles writes, "How can I strengthen the attraction of my new idea by hitching it directly to one or more of the five senses?"

How can you show your product in use? Can you demonstrate its ease of use?

117

chapter fourteen

D R. PAUL H. NYSTROM, OF COLUMBIA UNIVERSITY, WAS talking with me. "One thought I try to keep before my students all of the time," he declared; "it is that they should always be ready for change, but at the same time they should remember that change rarely comes as fast as they expect it."

In 1930, American Industry spent nearly $250,000,000 on its technical laboratories and there were at least a hundred times as many research organizations as there had been thirty years earlier. Patents were being granted at the rate of fifty thousand a year.

In the spring of that same year Andrew Mellon, at a meeting of the United States Chamber of Commerce, made this statement: "Anyone who has witnessed the new invention, the birth of a new industry—which has so vastly increased the wealth of the world and altered our entire mode of living within the memory of those present, cannot be discouraged about either the immediate or the distant future. The opportunities which have so multiplied in the last generation, are only the forerunners of perhaps greater ones, which will come as the result of forces now at work and constantly being discovered."

Mr. Mellon was referring more particularly to the advent of such inventions as the automobile and the radio receiving set. Not everyone can hope to be successful, however, in new dramatic industries. Fortunately, as Dr. Nystrom reminds us, change does not always come as rapidly as we expect it. Progress, for the most part, advances in short easy steps rather than by record-making leaps. Product innovations in a large degree consist merely of simple additions and subtractions. Adding an ink reservoir to a pen established a worldwide business for the Waterman family, but a promising addition need not be as novel as that. Somewhere in the past, the mere addition of an eraser to a pencil altered an industry. At times the addition of bright color has been enough to lift a product above competition.

Many products have been so long familiar that the public in a rather bored way regards them as old stand-bys. Their early appeal to the imagination has evaporated through long exposure, and yet even these cases may be far from hopeless. Simple additions may revive or expand the sales of old-timers in surprising measure.

Even in highly standardized industries, it is always possible that a variation will crop up to open larger markets than those previously enjoyed. Consider so basic a commodity as dogs! All present varieties have been evolved from some common wolf-like ancestor. But simple additions and subtractions have given the dog family a range of variation that provides satisfaction for every type of customer—one dog plus added watchfulness; another plus, special hunting ability; a third plus, an unusual color or shape. In a similar way this same plus or minus element applies to horses, cattle, flowers, vegetables, fruits-oranges plus extra juice, oranges minus seeds, etc. It stirs imagination to examine possibilities in this direction.

The suggestions in this chapter are few but they lead to answers to the general question, "What can I add to my product that will give it greater appeal to the public?"

ADD Performance. The fountain pen brought freedom from dipping one's pen repeatedly in ink, so this new writing instrument commanded as much as a hundred times the price of old-style pens. A clock plus an alarm added a new service to time-keepers. While this book is being written, a New York department store is advertising a comfortable chair which can be converted into a bed. With the arrival of high-compression automobile engines, low-priced gasolines were found unsatisfactorily noisy, and millions of car owners were willing to pay three cents extra to get gasoline plus ethyl to avoid the knock that frequently accompanied the use of cheaper fuel.

Additions which contribute to performance take many forms. Some are based merely on a passing fad or fashion but they reward the innovator handsomely just the same. When luxuriant walrus mustaches were in fashion, there was a ready market for coffee cups plus lip guards to keep the mustaches from dipping in. Perhaps it was about the same time that guards were added to razors and safety razors were born. These two simple additions remind us of a question, "What shortcoming in this product might be obviated by some simple addition?" Railroad travel by night was too uncomfortable to be popular until Mr. Pullman added beds to coaches. Now we have freight cars plus refrigeration, cars plus tanks to carry liquids which formerly could not be shipped in bulk. A furnace plus an automatic stoking device offers another example of marrying two products to overcome a basic drawback. A different type of wedding is that of a radio set to a phonograph; here compactness is gained through combining two instruments in one cabinet. A cigarette plus menthol overcomes the objection to "hot" smoke.

Perhaps you have also seen those cigarettes plus matches. You strike and light the end like a match. Recently a prominent scientist with whom I was visiting put one of his feet on the desk, raised his trouser leg, and revealed a sock plus a garter—a new type of elastic thread which was woven into the top of the sock held it snugly in place. Experimental socks of this type had been laundered fifty times and the rubber showed neither breakage nor loss of elasticity.

ADD Price Appeal. A most practical aim in business is the production of a really serviceable article at the lowest possible price. By aiming at a net profit of not over 2 1/2 percent, the A & P stores add price appeal which is hard for the customer to resist. In certain other lines a policy of selling at "cost plus 10 percent" serves to attract new customers.

As prices are lowered, the market widens. The classic example is our old friend, the Ford automobile. Another automobile manufacturer at the high-price end of the industry found that sixteen times as many people could be interested in a $3,000 automobile as in a $5,000 car. Similar possibilities of expansion face the electrical refrigerator and other high-priced articles as means are found to lower the selling price.

Another variant is supplied by the definite policy as to selling price. We see this employed in the one-price shoe or clothing store. We see it again in the "6 percent less than elsewhere" policy of R. H. Macy & Company. Often manufacturers set a certain retail price as their goal and then compel themselves to meet it. Recently I entered into a train conversation with a gentleman who was a tack manufacturer. He asked me my business, and when I told him, followed up with the question, "How would you promote the sale of tacks?" I replied that I would get up the best box of tacks I could to retail at 10 cents and then try to sell them through the Woolworth stores. "We did that a year ago," he replied, "and it's working fine."

ADD Youth Appeal. College students, some years ago, changed the trend in men's clothing by adopting the British type of suit which up to that time was popular in only a limited way. The president of one of the biggest tobacco companies tells me that college boys first popularized Turkish cigarettes and later the blended cigarette. Probably the collar-attached shirt, once considered so sloppy, was put over by its appearance on the college campus.

It is interesting to speculate as to how rapidly radio would have taken hold if thousands of mechanically minded boys had not bought parts from which they made the inexpensive sets of early days, for it was these amateur sets which introduced radio entertainment to the whole family and often to the neighbors. To achieve its maximum success, almost any product ought to have a strong appeal to youth.

ADD Name Appeal. "Club Breakfasts" and "Blue Plate Specials" have made many a restaurant menu a better drawing card. Rogers Peet can modify an army shoe and make it sound—oh, so much more fashionable—by christening it a "West Pointer." Some important questions to be considered in naming a product include these:

Is it easy to pronounce? A perfume named "Djer-Kiss" won national popularity in spite of the fact that many women called it "Didyerkiss" and "Jer-kiss." But perhaps sales would have risen still faster if the name had been less open to mispronunciation.

Can the name he shortened? A short name is usually easier to remember and easier to display. The name "Lux" on a package is relatively large and carries farther to the eye than would a name twice as long.

Any name which is inappropriate or suggestive of something different has hurdles to jump-for example, "Salada" sounds more like a salad dressing than a tea. And any member of the Smith or Jones family may well hesitate before he puts his name on a product, for greater individuality is advisable. However, good family names often appeal more to customers' imaginations than descriptive words. "Wanamaker's" probably attracts more customers than would "The New York Department Store," even though the latter offered better values.

Sometimes to old familiar names new secondary names may be added to refresh the customer's interest. For example, Maxwell House Coffee goes into a vacuum-sealed can and puts on its container the added words "VITA-FRESH Vacuum Package."

ADD *Luxury Appeal.* When Elmer J. Bliss copied expensive English custom-made shoes, he put a luxury appeal into Regal Shoes that competitors failed to match. A furniture maker offers inexpensive copies of museum pieces, specialty shops and department stores offer authentic copies of Parisian hats at a fraction of the cost of the originals, several rug manufacturers now offer at moderate prices copies of expensive Oriental rugs. If you can't cut down the price, perhaps the appearance of the product can be made more luxurious.

ADD *Health Appeal.* The electric refrigerator is being sold to some extent on the health appeal that it protects foods longer against spoilage. We see shoes plus flexible shanks and shoes plus reinforced arches to satisfy the desire for healthier feet. A chewing gum plus a laxative made one man's fortune.

But health appeal may be added without in the least changing the product. Simple changes in the factory may result in more sanitary manufacturing conditions. Once all cigars were made by hand, then a way was found to produce good cigars by automatic machinery. I was asked to help advertise a cigar which was probably the first to be produced in large volume by machinery. I had previously visited still larger plants where cigars were made by hand, and while every precaution was taken to assure cleanliness, one left these factories without having his desire for cigars any the keener. The machine-made cigar was a great improvement in this respect and it offered dramatic advertising possibilities. However, machine-made cigars continued to be advertised along old lines until George Washington Hill came out with his spectacular "No Spit" campaign for Cremo Cigars.

Shredded Wheat in its early days emphasized sanitary production and invited visitors to its factory at Niagara Falls. Another food manufacturer, some years ago, found it profitable to order his factory employees to put on fresh white gloves every morning so that this emphasis on cleanliness could be advertised.

Add Accurate Sizing. Not many years ago, starched collars in quarter sizes were first announced. Accurate sizing and special models for stout, stocky, and lean men were important factors in making ready-to-wear clothing acceptable to those who formerly would buy only custom-made suits and overcoats. In 1929 only a few stores could supply hats made specially for long or round heads. Now at least one manufacturer is supplying such models as part of his regular line. But accurate sizing is not confined to wearing apparel. The adjustable driver's seat in an automobile and greater variation in fountain pen sizes remind us that more accurate sizing may be possible in still other fields.

ADD Yearly Models. One of the most progressive manufacturers I know says, "We make our designers create at least two new models a year because this is the one sure way to keep them thinking constantly about improvements." Good idea, that; the old-fashioned business men made their product, established it, and then stood pat in positive fear that once the customer got acquainted with the goods he would resist change of any nature. Those days are gone forever.

The idea of bringing out yearly or periodical new models is applicable to more lines than clothing and automobiles. The success of Eastman Kodaks has been due in part to the steady appearance of improved models.

ADD Strength to Weak Features. The first manufacturer to knit extra reinforcements at the toe and heel of men's socks had a simple addition which appealed not only to the man who wore them, but to wives who darned. When the vacuum bottle business seemed nicely settled down, a new arrival appealed to imagination by offering all-steel construction which could not shatter. At twice the price of other bottles, it enjoyed good sales. The weak point in a check used to be the comparative ease with which a nimble hand could wash off the writing and raise the figures—but paper manufacturers discovered a way to foil the forger.

Glass had many weak points; it would not let in the ultra-violet rays-and a way was found to avoid that; it shattered— but it doesn't any more; it would not bend and spring back flat but now a product (though not true glass) is made which will curve and level out again. So a practical way to direct one's imagination is to look for the weak spots or characteristics and realize that some day they will be eliminated.

ADD Amateur Possibilities. Probably many of today's inventions which can now be used only by professional operators will soon be made available to the amateur. Shaving once required an almost professional touch. Not so many years ago photography required professional skill and equipment. A generation ago the automobile required a trained and many-sided technician at the wheel if a long trip was planned. The player piano made reasonably good music available to those whose hands were all thumbs. Today any amateur can make passable moving pictures. The sun lamp has become popular in the home as well as in the doctor's office. If the use of your product at present requires special skill, consider—as did George Eastman—the larger possibilities of the amateur market.

ADD Better Conditioning. Cigars remain fresh longer in Cellophane than when unwrapped in an open box. A food company advertised dated coffee, assuring the delivery of fresh goods to the customer. Candy manufacturers who sell nationally have suffered from the fact that they had to ship to distant points, for there was no way to keep chocolates from turning gray and spoiling. Local candy manufacturers operating their own stores not only deliver fresh goods daily to the consumer but can also offer chocolates with soft centers which will not ship well over long distances. Any product that is subject to spoilage may count on the certainty that some day that obstacle will be ended. Why not be first?

ADD Quicker Results. As life grows more complex we have less time per activity. So the oatmeal that used to require all-night cooking has been transformed into an oatmeal that can be cooked thoroughly in only three minutes.

One advertising agent makes sales records for food products by featuring quick recipes—women simply will not waste the time in the kitchen that they used to. High-speed machinery and high-speed automobile engines cater to the desire for quickness. Tabloid newspapers win huge circulations by enabling the reader to review the day's events at a gallop. Cameras must have fast lenses, fast film— followed by 6-hour developing and printing. We demand mastery of French or the tarapatch in five easy lessons, and an adequate library on a five-foot bookshelf.

ADD Adjustable Feature to suit the taste of the buyer. A suitcase recently designed has won popularity because it can be expanded or contracted to accommodate whatever the owner needs to carry on each individual trip. A straw hat has a flexible band that "gives," thus adjusting the hat to long or round skulls. A safety razor can be adjusted for a close or a light shave. A new type of woman's stocking has an adjustable top so that it can be adapted to the long, short or medium leg. Some products sell better when extra models are designed to fit small or large hands. Fountain pens offer a variety of points suited to different types of handwriting.

ADD Greater Beauty. This means: mechanical parts should be out of sight, lines and surfaces should be modern, projections must be eliminated, irregularities smoothed out, colors both stylish and acceptable, package and label modern. In some cases recognized style authorities should redesign or approve the new styles. Perhaps styles are too few in number to please every type of customer. On the other hand, there may be too many styles and these lead to confusion on the part of both merchant and customer in selecting the best for his own use.

ADD Product Individuality. Where new products come to succeed older ones, it seems curiously difficult to depart from the lines and appearance of the old-timer. It was a real struggle to develop the automobile to a point where it ceased to look like a carriage and took on its own individuality; some early automobiles even had whip sockets. And John Fitch might have occupied Fulton's place in history if, in 1787, he had been able to disregard the rowboat and equip his steamboat with revolving paddles instead of trying to use steam-propelled oars. No doubt some new inventions are more acceptable on account of their resemblance to products they aim to replace, but that advantage wears away and evolution is sure to lead to new individuality.

ADD Two-sex Appeal. Berets, for example, among hats, are worn by both men and women. Adding feminine smokers to masculine ones has expanded the market for cigarettes. London tobacconists offer special pipes and special cigars for women. If your wares appeal to one sex only, how can you make them attractive to both men and women?

INSIGHTS TO IMAGINATION:

Review Giles' questions, "What can I add to my product (or service) that will give it greater appeal to the public?

What shortcoming in this product (or service) may obviated by some simple addition?

Go through the sixteen categories Giles mentions. While not all of them will apply to your situation, pick the two or three most applicable. Study the question and let your mind wander. This is also a good time to ask your customers if there is anything they would like to see you add to your goods or services.

After implementing one or more changes (improvements), look at some of the other areas. See if any of the other categories make sense for your situation.

129 | subtraction works too

chapter fifteen

SALTED CODFISH IN THE EARLY NINETIES WAS DRY AND full of bones. When Gorton of Gloucester decided to specialize on packaged codfish, he took out the bones and this simple act of subtraction led to one of the biggest successes in the fish business. If simple additions work miracles in business, it is true that subtractions often result in equally happy innovations. For example:

SUBTRACT Seasonal Limitations. Coca-Cola and ginger ale have overcome the winter declines that occurred formerly in their sales. Ice cream has progressed in winter popularity by making known its food value. Strawberries and other "summer" fruits were once seasonal, but quick freezing and airplane delivery are doing away with that.

By developing rapid and inexpensive lenses, successful fall, winter, and rainy-day photography has been brought within the reach of nearly all. Manufacturers of style items find that preseason promotion increases their sales. Automobiles doubled both in mileage per year and in number of customers when inexpensive enclosed bodies made winter driving pleasant.

SUBTRACT Need of Attention. Here come to mind a host of automatic controls: the thermostat, the automatic stoker for furnaces, the automatic spark control on automobiles to eliminate the need to advance or retard ignition. An automatic focusing device on some cameras eliminates the need to calculate distance between the object to be photographed and the camera. The calculator built into some camera shutters tells you almost automatically what exposure to give the picture. A gasoline gauge on the dash of your car tells you automatically when to stop for five gallons more. Non-tarnishing radiators and headlights eliminate the need of frequent polishing.

Any device which requires servicing or frequent renewal of parts tends to be improved so as to overcome this handicap as time goes on. Creative imagination and determined effort to overcome such short-comings in present products will pave the way for new fortunes small and large.

SUBTRACT Bulk. Securing more output or better performance from smaller machines is another step in mechanical evolution. We see this principle at work even in our household contraptions and clothing. A light, compact typewriter successfully invades our homes, we are offered a camera which can be slipped into a vest pocket, progressively smaller radio sets replace the big cabinets of yesterday.

The opera hat was designed originally to tuck under the theater seat where a regular silk hat might be ruffed or smashed. This collapsible "stovepipe" died for a while, but it is staging a strong comeback. A rubber manufacturer has produced a full-size men's raincoat which can be rolled up into practically nothing at all and weighs only eighteen ounces. Another rubber manufacturer evolved the rubber minus shanks and heels for compactness. Now you can get a pair of women's rubbers which roll into a tiny ball and can be slipped into a small handbag.

Midget sizes are popular in many fields. They fit in with the basic needs which go with crowded living in apartments and smaller houses, and the need to crowd our many possessions into little space.

SUBTRACT Undesirables. To many, caffein is undesirable. Subtracting it from coffee opened a large market to Sanka and Kaffee Hag. Nicotine is equally undesirable to many others and a nice specialty business is enjoyed today by manufacturers of cigars and cigarettes from which almost all of the nicotine has been removed. The subtraction of the fattening elements of wheat results in a gluten bread which appeals to those who want to reduce.

INSIGHTS TO IMAGINATION:

Giles lists four categories where subtraction may be useful. Look at what you offer or would like to offer. Could you provide an entry level option to appeal to more people? What could you reduce or remove to make your product or service unique? Could you focus on a particular niche?

131

| # wanted: more originality in selling

chapter sixteen

O NE THURSDAY NOON IN DECEMBER, TWO HUNDRED OR more met at the weekly luncheon of the Sales Executives Club of New York. After we had eaten, two professors from New York University shared with us some discoveries they had made about salesmanship.

Professor Borden led off with an explanation. It seems that he and Professor Busse had listened to some twenty thousand sales interviews. Their object was to find out, if possible, those characteristics or methods which go hand in hand with successful selling and at the same time to learn why it is that some selling interviews are sheer waste of time for salesman and buyer alike. These two men spent seven and a half years in this study. They sat beside purchasing agents, independent merchants, and chain store buyers, listening to commercial salesmen for hours on end. But even that did not satisfy them. They listened also to other types of sellers— from Congressmen trying to sell new bills to their opponents down to employees trying to sell new business ideas to their employers. Each interview was carefully recorded; then all twenty thousand were reviewed to learn what lessons might be extracted. (Since writing this chapter I find that Messrs, Busse and

Borden have put their survey into a book called *How to Win an Argument*.)

WHEN SALESMEN STUMBLE

Facts gathered in this way deserve more than passing attention, for probably no other study of selling has been so far-reaching or has covered so many different fields. From stenographic notes taken that day at the Hotel Roosevelt it appears that nine out of every ten salesmen make certain common mistakes day in and day out, and year after year. Borden gave six general, sure-fire Don'ts in selling. And—so that you can see how common they are—here is his list:

"Principle No. 1. During the course of the sales argument, above everything else, watch out that you don't do too much of the talking yourself.

"Principle No. 2. During the course of the sales interview, never interrupt your prospect.

"Principle No. 3. ("This is really a corollary to one and two," explained Borden.) During the course of the sales argument, watch out that you never unconsciously slip into an argumentative manner or one that is belligerent or overpositive.

"Principle No. 4. During the opening phase of a selling interview, inquire first and attack afterwards. When your prospect opens with an objection, don't hop in and say, 'You're wrong!' Ask him to tell you a little more fully why he thinks he is right. If you do so he fires off half his ammunition first, so that in the decisive phase of the interview he tends to listen and that is something of unbelievable importance. His aggressive attitude becomes rather that of receptiveness— perhaps through exhaustion.

"Principle No. 5. During the course of a sales interview when your prospect has expressed an objection, repeat it in your own words. Do this even before thinking of an answer. If you don't, your prospect is never content that you have understood his objection. He turns over in his mind some new way of repeating the same objection.

"Principle No. 6. After you have inquired and restated and you seek to launch the killing thrust, at that time it is best that you boil things down and concentrate on one key issue. The thing to do is to nail one point to the board. If he wanders, bring him back to that key issue."

SELLING "IN REVERSE"

Professors Borden and Busse amplified these Don'ts in considerable detail. They reenacted actual sales interviews from their collection of case histories. But as I listened, it seemed to me that the one stupendous finding of their study they failed to mention at all. I refer to the apparent fact that most salesmen would actually do better to turn their entire selling practice upside down— do exactly the opposite from what is expected of them, and what they are too often taught and urged to do.

The average salesman thinks that he must be the talker and the buyer must remain a listener. He seeks to smother objections even before the listener has a chance to voice them. He has a certain selling talk which he must get off his chest before the buyer has a chance to utter a word. The buyer is to be overwhelmed with everything in the selling arsenal— arguments, claims, facts, manufacturing data, figures, pleas. Borden admitted that many salesmen question the wisdom of his advice on this point, but he says it fairly shouts out from twenty thousand actual selling interviews.

And interruptions! The average salesman is so eager to answer objections and otherwise bend the prospective customer to his will that interruptions keep popping out of him. Salesmen gradually are learning the folly of high-pressure methods, but not so many are ready to adopt a low-tension attitude. They think it is necessary to act alert and on the job. In this they may be right, but the alert mental condition must not be too apparent to the buyer. As for avoiding "the argumentative manner or one that is belligerent or over-positive," the salesman is often selected and trained to have this very characteristic. He is hired in preference to some one else because of his more positive manner, and often is encouraged

135

by his employers to develop this still further. On top of that, he sees that all the salesmen portrayed in books and on the stage are the embodiments of positive speech and strong personality.

Finally, isn't it the most natural thing in the world to pack into your closing talk all the arguments you can muster? — all the manufacturing data you can recall? —all the inducements you can possibly think of? Who ever heard of throwing most of them away and focusing the talk on one point? Yes; Busse and Borden's advice would turn most selling upside down. They prove that it pays to be contrary. If this is true, there is no department of business where originality is more needed and promises to pay better than in selling.

"DARING" THE BUYER

Many salesmen let their imaginations carry them in the wrong direction— for example, in meeting objections. Some salesmen have the habit of deciding even before meeting the buyer just what his objection will be. They try to handle the interview so that the prospect gets no chance to express his objection and this misapplied imagination results either in the buyer's conviction that his objection is valid or in a feeling of irritation at being forced to remain silent throughout the interview.

A salesman of automobile accessories, whose income runs into five figures even in bad years, proved that originality pays in meeting price objections. His line is high-priced and objections on that ground are common. One day he decided to stop pussy-footing about prices and raise the price objection himself, before the customer had a chance to do so. He selected for his first test a hard-shelled prospect, a Scotchman at driving a bargain. The salesman's opening remark was, "I came to see you about taking our line." Here he paused and eyed the victim appraisingly; then deliberately, and with something of a taunt in his voice, he added, "but it will cost you a lot of money."

The subject of his experiment blinked a little and reddened. "Well," he blurted, striking the bait like a trout, "what of it? Do you think I'm afraid to spend a lot of money?" After that, the salesman dodged the price objection no more; he found that by bringing it up at the start, it had a way of evaporating from the buyer's mind.

This contrary approach— a deliberately original one— is used effectively by some of the ablest salesmen. There was the salesman who found that buyers commonly preferred to get his type of merchandise from a factory nearer at hand. He opens his canvass with a dare: "Mr. Jones, *if distance is no barrier to you*, I'd like to talk about the possibility of our doing business together."

Oftener than not, the answer comes, "I don't see why a few miles should stand in the way if you have something really worth listening to."

Some years ago, a prominent tire manufacturer had a run of bad merchandise through his factory. Usual inspections and tests failed for some unknown reason and practically a whole year's output was below standard. The trouble did not show up until the tires were sold and had been run a few thousand miles. The defect was remedied as quickly as possible, but salesmen had tough going with dealers who were listening to so many complaints. In reselling the dealers, one salesman stood out among the rest like a red danger flag on an ice pond. The executives called him in to explain how he did it and found that one little piece of originality accounted for his success. "They tell me our tires were rotten last year," he said calmly, "and I reply, 'Sure; I know it—and they were worse than that—they were terrible? Then I tell them what we've done to remedy the situation both in making better tires and in providing new promotion material to get business again."

This man had no arguments or facts different from those supplied to the other salesmen. But he had added one original touch— he not only agreed quickly with the buyer's complaint but went him one better. And the more he admitted "those tires were terrible," the more likely the dealer was to say, "Oh, I don't think they were quite that bad."

137

This matter of meeting objections is worth special attention because the salesman who knows how to uncover and handle them has pretty much all he needs to sell well. A letter, booklet, or advertisement may present a selling talk even better than does the average salesman, but the printed word cannot always anticipate the objections that will come up. Salesmen can. So a salesman is known by the way in which he overcomes objections. Borden and Busse believe that stifling an objection or trying to answer it in a perfunctory way fastens the obstacle in the prospect's mind that much more strongly; the buyer may seem satisfied with the answer but actually he continues to mull it over in his mind and from that point on his listening becomes a mere pretense.

IMAGINATION VS. WILL POWER

The "strong-arm" salesman often floats from job to job and ends up a failure— all because he has not enough imagination. He relies on dogged insistence and will power, but dealers manage somehow to avoid buying. He is all "me and my product" instead of "you and your needs." Compare the two methods— that of willful, argumentative selling versus that of stirring imagination through pleasant images.

Mr. Strong-arm's proposal is about like this: "I want to sell you some typewriters. You need our make. The prices and terms are right. Our typewriter is better than any of this junk you have here. Sign on this dotted line."

Mr. Imagination says: "In a store as attractive and well-situated as yours, I believe you could sell a lot of our typewriters. Many people don't buy a typewriter without at least looking at ours and it gives a mighty fine demonstration. You may not think you are losing sales, but people look in your windows and when they fail to see our typewriter among the others they assume you don't carry it and walk on. Some of the best business houses in town such as A, B, and C use only our standard model. Lots of students in such schools as D, E, and F use our portables."

Notice that Mr. Strong-arm sets out to enforce his will on the prospective customer. Most dealers resent this. Strong-arm tries so hard to sell that he fails to point out the resale possibilities of the typewriters in any graphic way. Strong-arm does not hesitate to slam the typewriters the dealer carries, regardless of the fact that in so doing he criticizes the dealer's judgment.

Just a little imagination is needed to turn the same material into a really attractive presentation. Mr. Imagination remembers to put himself in the listener's place. The dealer is not interested in buying—that costs money and offers no reward in itself. No; the profitable and desirable store activity is that of selling. So the imaginative salesman talks to the dealer about selling typewriters and the dealer listens with both ears, for there is profit in each sale. The imaginative salesman talks about making more customers rather than putting in more idle stock.

What thought or picture will appeal most to the imagination of the buyer? Discover this and you have the surest key to a sale. The most practical imagination a salesman can have is that which enables him to capture the imagination of the customer. Compared to the complicated selling talks that are common, these appeals to the imagination are often surprisingly simple. Take the case of another salesman who sells high-priced clothing. He has discovered that the most effective appeal he can make is that of lodging a picture in the mind of the buyer—a picture of conducting a store which attracts more high-grade customers. He says to the dealer, "You certainly have an attractive store here, but what are you doing to get more high-grade business?" The dealer answers either that he does not get as much high-grade business as he would like or he may answer that he already has about all the high-grade trade he can reasonably expect. If this is the reply, the salesman says, "But, of course, you could take care of still more high-grade trade." The only possible answer is yes.

This salesman continues to paint a picture of more and more high-grade customers coming in for more and more high-grade clothing. He points to this as the natural result of featuring high-priced clothing, with its high-grade woolens and superior styling. He reminds the merchant that these high-grade garments offer not only more profit per sale, but that they are bought by high-grade customers who do not wear one suit threadbare before buying another. Well, the merchant simply hates to admit either to himself or to the salesman that he cannot qualify as a high-grade merchant, and if a sale is at all possible this approach usually makes it.

The cases related here are drawn from commercial salesmanship. But the same principles apply to the school-teacher trying to "sell" her principal on giving her a higher class. They apply to the wife trying to "sell" her husband the idea of buying a washing machine, and to the elevator boy trying to "sell" the starter on giving him a day off.

There may be objections to meet in each case, a difference of viewpoint to adjust, but the need is always to "sell" by handling the transaction from the listener's standpoint—not your own.

Insights to Imagination:

While the six principles outlined by Professors Borden and Busse have been modified over the years, they still hold tremendous value.

What contrary approach can you use in sales efforts?

Review the story of the tire salesman. Do you have one salesperson or store that is more successful than the others? If so, that is great news. Ask what they are doing differently. Apply it to your other salespeople or locations. Watch your results grow exponentially.

While typewriters are no longer a staple of our lives, there are great lessons to be gleaned from the story. You and your needs is still the major component of successful selling and communication today. See how you can incorporate it in everything you do.

Giles writes: "The dealer is not interested in buying—that costs money and offers no reward in itself. No; the profitable and desirable store activity is that of selling."

Take this statement and see how you can apply it to your venture. Is your sales presentation geared toward selling what you offer or helping your client sell more of what they offer?

How can you "sell" by handling the transaction from the listener's standpoint—not your own?

143 | one small improvement may change everything

ONE DAY WHILE LUNCHING WITH O. H. BLACKMAN, NOW at Stanford University, we let our minds speculate at random about the changes we thought would come in business. Among other ideas which "Black" advanced was the one that there would be some getting away from the widespread mania for standardization. Probably the worship of standardization reached its height during the World War. It was useful beyond question to have guns, trucks, bolts and nuts and other supplies, and spare parts highly standardized, but Blackman questioned the commercial peacetime value of making different brands of shoes, silverware, tires, and gasoline so much alike. He deplored the waste of sending out salesmen who were forced to talk in a similar way about products of almost identical specifications and appearance and which were sold at the same prices and on the same terms.

Only the day before, I had attended a training class of new salesmen hired by a company known the world over. The head of the technical department in a talk to these recruits calmly admitted that their product was no better and no worse than four or five rivals'. He said there was not even one small point of superiority which they could put before the dealers they called on. It is in competitive situations of this kind that the price wars are hottest and profits most uncertain. Here salesmen must sell against sharp difficulties.

Where goods are specialties, or embody a specialty touch, competition is usually less keen and there is a better chance of maintaining fair prices and reasonable profits. On the other hand, the specialty cannot always enjoy the mass market which is open to the standardized staple. So perhaps the most interesting possibilities lie before that staple which has just enough of the specialty touch to stand out among competitors. A few years ago I wrote that no one could expect to advertise eggs successfully because eggs were so highly standardized. I speculated on the possibility of adding extra vitamins to eggs so that some egg grower would have a specialty touch. Now that is actually happening, it is possible to produce eggs having extra vitamin D content by irradiating the hens. So there hardly seems to be a staple which cannot be given some individuality, if only the search is kept up long enough.

FROM SOAP TO SHIPS

Fifty years ago soaps were highly standardized, there being only a few varieties. When competition between soap makers grew keener, greater variation came in. The soap field still has its price wars, but the specialty touch seems to be alleviating that difficulty. Imagination has created new soap specialties which have appealed in turn to the imagination of the buyer.

Instead of only two or three forms of soap-one for toilet, one for clothes and dishes, and perhaps a harsh scouring soap, the housewife is offered today: Soap plus naphtha— for extra help in cleaning clothes. Soap plus flake form— for convenience and gentle cleansing of silk stockings. Soap plus dye— with which she can redye under-things. Soap plus carbolation— to eliminate body odor. Soap plus tar— for shampooing. Soap plus olive oil— for that schoolgirl complexion. Soap plus the ability to float— can't sink to the bottom of the bathtub. Soap plus liquidity— for convenience in wash-rooms. Soap plus abrasives— to get out grime that penetrates pores and gets under the nails.

Soap in powder form— dissolves instantly in hot water. All of which offers proof that Blackman's idea was sound. When we examine competitive products which have looked alike for years, we find that consumers become so indifferent to the many similar brands that specialty touches are advisable to establish individuality. During the past twenty years automobile lubricating oils have struggled more and more to individualize themselves by featuring certain processes, crudes, colors, and other variations in manufacture. The automobile owner shows considerable indifference about oils that all look alike, feel alike, and are priced alike. Even in ocean travel there has been a growing recognition of the importance of the specialty touch. This shows in the advertising of the different steamship lines in 1933. Here are some of the specialty touches which are being featured:

French line— French cuisine, French smartness.

Hamburg-American— stabilized ships that roll less.

Cunard— Cunard traditions, expert seamanship.

North German Lloyd— fastest ships to cross the Atlantic.

White Star—owns world's biggest ship.

Canadian Pacific—has liners with 27-foot state-rooms and sails over the shortest route.

Once there were only a few kinds of restaurants. Today, within a one-mile radius of Times Square in New York you find such varied eating places as the restaurant specializing in sea food, the place strong on salads and desserts, the old-time chophouse where you can summon thick steaks and titanic portions of ham and eggs, the armchair lunch specializing in egg sandwiches and baked apples, the hotel grill with orchestra and dance floor, the drugstore lunch counter, the delicatessen where you can get smoked sturgeon and cervelat, the tea room, the oyster bar, the saloon-like place where you eat at a bar, and restaurants specializing in Italian,

Chinese, Greek, Japanese, German, Hungarian, Armenian, French, or Hindu cooking.

Wouldn't filling stations and shoe stores be more interesting if they, too, offered greater variety? The specialized restaurant may have a limited appeal, but its customers are more loyal because they get exactly what they want. It often pays better to have a sharp appeal to a few customers than a limited appeal to a large group.

ORIGINALITY FOR WIDOWS

A friend, who prefers to remain anonymous, is a welfare worker who helps many people get to their feet again after losing a job or meeting with financial disaster in some form. One of her greatest fields of usefulness has been among indigent widows and old folks who cannot easily get work. Speaking of widows left with little cash and small children, she says: "Their first inclination is to seek employment in some field which is already crowded. This same general tendency you will find among young men and young women seeking work for the first time. Probably it is because these jobs are the more familiar ones. These highly standardized vocations usually offer poorer pay than some of the more specialized activities." The average widow who must go to work thinks of clerking in a department store or gift shop, acting as hostess in a tea room, or helping the local librarian. For such positions there is usually a long waiting list. Having no special experience to bring to these jobs, the untrained woman has little chance of succeeding. This welfare worker has a favorite list of questions she asks of women in such a predicament. Among them are these:

Is there any one thing you do unusually well?

What is your hobby?

At what subjects did you get your best marks in school or college?

What activities do you enjoy better than any others?

Answers to these and related questions often supply a key to selecting an occupation which will be far more remunerative than clinking a cash register or selling notions. Sometimes a nice specialty business is established.

"Is there anything you do unusually well?" After thinking a while, one widow replied, "My friends tell me that they never tasted soup as good as mine." She was urged to build up a specialty business in soups, and ended up with a long list of local customers who took her soups once, twice or thrice a week on a regular schedule. Many women make pin money specializing in one food product which they make particularly well— from Scotch scones to homemade chocolates.

"What is your hobby?" Another widow was fond of outdoor games and very proficient at them. Now she runs a playground for young children and is happier at it and making more money than she ever could by doing clerical work for the local gas company— which position she was about to accept before the specialty was suggested to her.

"At what subjects did you get your best marks in school or college?" A widow who liked all sorts of laboratory work was placed in a dentist's office where she had a grand time and earned more money than if she had accepted the first position which was offered to her— that of a tearoom hostess.

"What activities do you enjoy better than any others?" "I enjoy my flower garden," was one reply, "and have wonderful luck with plants and flowers." It had not occurred to this woman that she could make a living by selling plants and giving gardening advice to other women in her locality who liked flowers, too, but did not have her "luck."

At the entrance to a large public park stand so many more bootblacks that there cannot possibly be enough work for one in three. During 1931, the unemployed rushed to sell apples on the streets— most of them at meager earnings even when the idea was new and novel. Here and there some of these men who were all doing the same thing began to see the light and look for work having more of a specialty touch. Such opportunities are not rare. One man with only a razor blade sharpener for capital went from house to house sharpening dull blades. Others washed cars and pet animals—tasks which the average person detests and is only too glad to get off his hands. One man offered to clean drains, tighten faucets, replace worn washers sources of annoyance not great enough to justify calling in the plumber but ones which the householder was glad to have attended to.

A Baltimore baking company runs fourteen cut rate stores specializing in stale bread. On the front of his stores are signs reading: "Day Old Bread One-Half Price." A Newark baker jumped sales 15 percent within a few days by offering bread extra rich in vitamin D. Each 18-ounce loaf is said to contain more D than two teaspoonfuls of standard cod liver oil. A Massachusetts beverage maker offers a ginger ale containing vitamin C.

An Illinois grocer disposed of odds and ends of vegetables—turnips, parsnips, okra, celery, parsley, pepper, etc. — by making up a special "Soup Assortment" in Cellophane bags to sell for ten cents.

"FORD ADVISES JOBLESS"

Such is a headline from the New York Times of April 26, 1933. And the item reads, "Henry Ford believes that one thing people should learn from the depression 'is that necessity of creating their own business, no matter how small, instead of waiting for someone to give them a job. Everybody ought to have that in mind, because there are too many out of employment to provide jobs for all,' he said."

Yes, Mr. Ford, but how? The farmer who sells eggs direct to the consumer at a price lower than that asked by the grocer may make out well. But how about the grocery clerk who then loses his job because the grocery store business falls off? How about the jobless manufacturer? He may be outmaneuvered by competitors and have to quit. How about the drug clerk who loses his job? Should he peddle talcum powder from door to door?

Mr. Ford's advice, if complete as stated, leaves the reader high and dry. It is too much like the generality, "Stop worrying." Perhaps he had in mind the specialty jobs that could be created by using a little imagination. It is interesting to note the odd jobs mentioned by the University of Wisconsin in a bulletin printed to help students make money. From the *Readers' Digest*: "Among the emergency occupations it lists are: Skunk-hunting at night in automobiles (the skunk's eyes glisten in the headlights and can be seen at distances up to 600 feet), repairing cracked pools, setting up concrete bird baths, making teeter-totters for children, washing pet dogs (one man built up a nice little business, the book says), installing additional shut-off cocks, putting in disappearing stairs to attics, catching escaped pet canary birds, gathering up old magazines and selling them for two cents apiece, collecting odd-shaped rocks to sell to city people for rock gardens, reconstructing dry wells, repainting wheelbarrows, and rearranging basements."

149

Passing fads or temporary conditions may point the way to specialties which lead to new vocations or provide more sales. Ely Culbertson, writing in the American Magazine, says: "In a few years bridge has developed into a great industry, with a turnover of more than a hundred million dollars. More than 2,000 people make a profession of teaching bridge and nearly half a million people took lessons from them last year. It is estimated that about 20,000,000 Americans play the game. More than 100 bridge books are published yearly, and until the publishers of other books demanded recently that books on bridge be classified separately, they headed all the lists of nonfiction best sellers."

In 1932, the amateur show business was another booming activity that provided work for printers of programs, makers of electric light bulbs, costumers, ushers. Over 14,000 amateur groups put on plays of their own.

In 1933, there were 200,000 retailers featuring Mickey Mouse merchandise of one kind or another. A single trade paper carried advertisements of a dozen manufacturers of Mickey Mouse clothing, all specially licensed by Walt Disney, creator of the movie rodent. The Mickey Mouse name appeared also on pottery and jewelry.

Just before beer was restored to a thirsty public, a manufacturer sent his sales to a new level by putting his jelly into beer mugs.

In other cases the specialty touch may be spread with a lavish hand over such a standardized affair as the railroad coach. Reports Forbes': "As the Florida Year-Round Clubs Special, crack New York-to-Miami flier, pulled out of Pennsylvania Station one evening in November, passengers wandered into a car whose like they had never seen before—a 'recreation car.' Some rode the electric horse in the gymnasium; some browsed in the library; a few splashed in the miniature swimming pool, ten feet long, six feet wide, and two feet deep. If they preferred moving pictures, a show was going on in a car—wide corridor; later, the room was cleared, and passengers might dance to the tunes of a three-piece orchestra. If they still weren't satisfied, passengers found expert instructors in bridge and backgammon.

"Commuters, too, have a new convenience. For those who like to sleep to the last minute, a 'breakfast car' is running on one of the N.Y., N. H. & H. suburban trains into New York. A business man supplied the idea; the New Haven furnished him with a day-coach to carry it out. He transformed it into a traveling cafeteria, with a counter, red-topped stools, curtains, and pine-board paneling. Club breakfasts ranged in price from 30 cents to 75 cents. On return trips, just before dinner, business also is good—a real surprise to the management."

Then, too, a specialty touch may be supplied by a policy rather than something which shows in the merchandise or the stock arrangement or the store appearance. R. H. Macy's policy of selling only for cash leads to lower pricing through the elimination of losses due to bad charge accounts.

It is the policy of the General Tire and Rubber Company to concentrate on the quality market and not compete with other tire makers for unprofitable original equipment business from car manufacturers. Relatively small, but very efficient, the General Tire Company is the one prominent tire manufacturer which has paid dividends equal to three times its original capital.

Sometimes a specialty may be born from the marriage of two dissimilar stores or jobs. Up in Montreal a barber shop married a tailoring establishment. When you go in you can take off your clothes; the tailor gives you a dressing gown, then you go through a door into the barber shop, sit down for a haircut or shave while your suit is being pressed. Out you come fresh all over time and bother saved.

In business we are often too imitative. We copy successful products and methods and the result is that consumers are bewildered or made indifferent by the sameness of rival offerings. We think too much of the standardized jobs. Whatever we do, there is always room for a specialty touch. Since no two people, flowers, or mountains are exactly alike, nature must abhor standardization. Each one of us is a specialty; each one can put some unique stamp of originality in his or her work. That's where profits and satisfaction come from.

INSIGHTS TO IMAGINATION:

What can you do to make your products or services embody a specialty touch? Focus on what makes your offering unique. If you are having difficulty, ask your current clients for help.

If you are thinking of launching your own business, study the questions Giles' friend poses.

Is there any one thing you do unusually well?

At what subjects did you get your best marks in school or college?

What activities do you enjoy better than any others?

Remember, Giles' closing words from this chapter. "Each one of is a specialty, each one can put some unique stamp of originality in his or her work. That's where profits and satisfaction come from."

chapter eighteen

DURING THE DIFFICULT YEAR OF 1932, I TALKED WITH A gray-haired visitor from Boston. He made a good living by selling ideas. His talents ranged from creating a novel new penny confection to organizing an insurance sales force. As we parted, he said, "And don't overlook the obvious; people get so snarled up in their problems that they often fail to see obvious solutions that lie right under their noses."

Some years ago a grocery clerk was cutting cheese. You don't have to be very old to remember the kind—a huge round American cheese, kept under a glass cover like those stuffed birds on the mantelpieces of the eighties. When you asked for a pound, the clerk lifted the glass bell and cut off a piece, estimating the weight by its heft. While the glass was off, the cheese was exposed to air and dust and picnicking flies. If sales were slow, the cheese might begin to crumble before the last was gone. The chief protection of the cheese in its trip from factory to grocery store was a tough rind—you had to buy the rind along with the cheese, and it was that much waste and annoyance.

One day the grocery clerk had a thought. It was an obvious one that might come to anyone with eyes in his head—but it is often such ideas that build fortunes. This is what imagination suggested: Why not put cheese in sanitary packages? That would end several shortcomings in old-fashioned American cheese—such as:

Inaccurate weight—when you asked for a pound of the packaged cheese you would get it—exactly.

Slow service—the packaged cheese could be taken immediately from the shelf.

Rind elimination—no rind would be needed to protect the packaged cheese.

Flies kept off—for they could not possibly enter a sealed package.

Spoilage eliminated—no crumbling through exposure to air.

No filching of free samples by hangers around the grocery store.

This grocery clerk's name was J. L. Kraft, and every time you see or eat Kraft cheese let it remind you that a simple, obvious idea may lead to wealth.

THE LADY PROM FRANCE

One day in 1847, a woman entered the shop of a Boston chemist. She asked the proprietor if he had any vanilla extract like that she used when she lived in France. She wanted it to flavor her desserts. The chemist could not help her then. As a matter of fact, lemon was the only flavoring extract being used in America, although some flavoring was done with plain vanilla beans which were put in little bags and used more or less like tea balls. Well, what obvious thoughts did that experience suggest to the Boston chemist?

He decided that if vanilla extract could be made in France, it could be duplicated here.

He saw that such an extract would be far more convenient to use than plain vanilla bean.

So the chemist, Joseph Burnett, did something that was perfectly obvious—he experimented until he had a good vanilla extract. People called him original and with reason, for his was the first vanilla extract in the United States. Business prospered on the new product and it remains a leader in grocery stores of to-day. Every drop of Burnett's Vanilla which your wife or mother or sister puts into her cake batter celebrates again the possibilities of the obvious.

During the gold rush of '49 when prospectors headed for California and the Northwest, a farmer boy in the horde made an obvious observation; he noticed that prospectors who found gold in satisfactory quantities were few and far between. He, too, had planned to dig gold, but in that particular year such a plan was in no way original. As he continued musing he had three quick thoughts—all obvious:

(1)All prospectors had to eat. (2)Provisioning facilities were poor. (3)Selling food to prospectors gave surer promise of gold than did the use of picks, shovels, and cradles.

This original-minded farm boy was Philip D. Armour, and every time you slice an Armour ham let it impress upon you again the gold that may often be mined from plain obviousness. Yes; the obvious is often the most original thing to do—and the most practical.

An automobile dealer in Massachusetts wanted to compile a list of local car owners to whom he would send letters in an effort to sell his gasoline, his lubricating oil, and his tires. The usual way of getting such a roster is to buy it from some company specializing in mailing lists, or gather local names and addresses from the telephone directory. Both these methods are all right but may involve considerable waste. This dealer had an original thought even though it was decidedly obvious: He asked his daughter to sit out front and watch the cars go by. When a license number passed the garage four times it was transferred to a final list of people to whom the letters went. Thus was wastage avoided, for every name was that of some neighboring motorist who regularly passed by.

The owner of a small and exclusive hotel wanted to enlarge his restaurant trade. One day he needed two more waitresses. His newspaper advertisement brought thirty applicants. It was only a coincidence that six of the thirty had red hair, but the hotel man already had two waitresses with red tops, and the thought struck him that he might individualize his restaurant and make it talked about if every waitress was a redhead. He had redecorating to do and he made it harmonize with the waitresses' hair. Trade grew. People remarked, "How original!" but "How obvious" they might have said with equal truth.

A LETTER FEOM THE SHERIFF

Robert Collier had an interesting experience with obvious thinking. A hospital wanted to raise money. Collier says: "When starting a new drive, they usually planned a series of six or eight letters to their whole list. But, knowing that after the first letter, every recipient could tell from a glance at the corner card what was coming, and harden his heart accordingly, they used a bit of psychology. If you were on their list, the first letter you'd receive would probably be from the Sheriff's office, with a big badge in the corner of the envelope and the card of the Sheriff's office staring you in the face.

"Now your conscience may be so clear that getting a letter from the Sheriff will give you no thrill, but most people's are not. So that envelope was opened eagerly, and when it was found that all the Sheriff wanted was to get you to contribute to the Hospital fund, the relief on the part of many was so great that they gladly gave a contribution.

"The next letter in the series might come from a Justice of the Supreme Court, then from a prominent banker, a clergyman, a doctor and so on, ending with a final appeal from the Hospital itself."

Obvious thinking may even be used in such an original way that special trains stop to pick you up as a passenger. Another friend, Frank W. Lovejoy, a sales executive with one of the largest oil refiners, tells of an obvious thing he did late one night when in a middle-sized city between New York and Chicago. A local sales meeting had kept him overtime and made him miss the train for

Chicago, where he was due the next day. Arriving at the depot, he asked if there was another train before morning.

"No," was the reply, "that is, only a nonstop train that carries the mail."

"Well," suggested Lovejoy, "perhaps you could get them to pick me up."

"Oh no; that would be impossible! Why I've been here sixteen years and I never heard of such a thing being done with that train."

Finally Lovejoy got the station master to telegraph headquarters requesting a stop. Much to that worthy man's astonishment the request was granted. The mail train thundered in, pulled up short, and a train man hopped off expecting nothing less than the president of the railroad or the President of the United States. Looking at Lovejoy in amazement, he said, "Well, I've been on this run for over twenty years but nothing like this ever happened before."

A prominent outdoor advertising man, H. Belden Joseph, had to devise some painted signs to be erected in New York for Gold Medal Flour. That city, like most other large ones, is a group of cities within a city. It contains a Jewish city, an Irish city, an Italian city, an Armenian city, an African-American city, a Chinese city. Many of these groups are intensely loyal to their own race or nationality. Joseph got up some signs reading, "Mrs. Smith says Gold Medal makes better bread," "Mrs. Brown says Gold Medal makes better pastry," etc. That was simple and unlike any other outdoor advertising. Then Joseph plussed his original idea with a bit of obviousness that made it still more original. In the Jewish sections of New York, he changed the texts to "Mrs. Cohen says Gold Medal makes better bread," "Mrs. Levy says Gold Medal makes better pastry." In the Italian sections he shifted to "Mrs. Aucello says," "Mrs. Corsi says," while over in the Irish section it was Mrs. Clancy and Mrs. O'Rourke. This Joseph idea, like so many other obvious ones, resulted in originality which cost not a penny more than would have been spent on something commonplace.

Solomon Bernato Joel, son of an English bar-keeper, wanted to enter the diamond business in South Africa. At that time the Boers would not tell strangers the names of natives from whom they bought their precious stones. Joel was stumped-until something obvious occurred to him. One day he told a Boer diamond merchant that he needed a horse immediately and would pay a premium to get one. An old nag was offered at a fancy price and Joel bought it. "Came the dawn," as they used to say in the movies, and Joel left on his trip. Once beyond the town lines he loosened the reins over the horse's neck and let him go his own sweet way. Like a milk horse on a familiar route, Joel's guide stopped at every place where his former master had paused to buy diamonds. "From then on," reports the War Cry, "Joel bought, until the diamond business was entirely in his hands." Talk about business originality based upon the obvious!

OBVIOUS JOB HUNTING

If there is one place above others where originality is needed in business it is in job hunting. Here, too, the obvious thing is often the most original.

Brock Mathewson, prominent in advertising circles, likes to tell about a young job hunter who gave him a busy six weeks. This twenty-year-old youth applied for a position without making any special impression, but that was only the beginning. During the six weeks that followed he kept up his bombardment. Every working day Mathewson received either a postcard or a letter from this persistent youngster— on each card would be typed another reason why the job hunter thought he would make good. Each letter suggested a plan or idea by which Mathewson's publication might get more advertising. The cub was applying for a job as a copy writer, and there were ho openings of that kind. There was, however, a vacancy of a much better sort. The New York State representative had recently resigned. At the end of the six weeks Mathewson decided that such a persistent person ought to make a good salesman. He gave this better job to the young man and says that his judgment was vindicated.

During the past twelve years I have talked with many job hunters. For two years I headed the copy department of a large advertising agency. Here, if anywhere, you would expect to find applicants showing a bit of originality. But, no; as a class, these men and women whose success depended entirely on their inventiveness showed little of that quality in promoting themselves. Employers in many other lines tell me it is the same with them; original methods in seeking employment are rare.

To begin with, the job hunter makes little or no study of the companies from which he seeks employ. That makes him a mere pleader, with seemingly little interest in anything but a pay envelope.

He readily accepts the old stall, "I'll file your name, and if anything turns up I'll get in touch with you."

He often has only vague ideas about what he really wants to do.

He fails to follow up his visit properly.

Now, it is obvious that any applicant for a position has a better chance if he makes some definite preparation for the interview. I knew a salesman who wanted employment with a certain food manufacturer. Before calling, he talked about this food specialty and its makers with six grocers; he asked several of his wife's friends what they thought about the product; he ate some himself; he learned all he could about competitive products. Once in the sales manager's office, there was not much doubt that he would make an unusually favorable impression. If he did not land a job that day he might do so later on. Such preparation requires no genius—only an appreciation of the value of the obvious.

After his first interview, an applicant for a job should have a good idea as to (1) whether the opening is really one that interests him and (2) just what kind of a follow-up will be effective with the man who does the employing. But too many regard the initial interview as the only one that counts. Sometimes that is really the case, but often it is not. Even if the vacancy is to be filled that day, the applicant has a chance to walk around the block a few times after his interview and consider what else he can say to help his chances. A telephone call costs only a nickel. And the better the follow-up, the greater one's chance of getting a position later on or in some other department of the business.

OBVIOUS THOUGHTS POSSIBLE TO ALL

So we see that one of the most hopeful facts in business is that the obvious thing to do is often over-looked by others. Asking, "What is the obvious need in this job?—in this store?—in this factory?—in this bank?" may lead to interesting results.

B. Altaian & Company wanted to know what items sell best in a January sale. They did the obvious—asked questions of 30,000 charge customers. On the questionnaire were listed 71 kinds of merchandise with three prices opposite each. From the answers received they planned a sale which was geared exactly in mesh with the desires of their trade.

A man whose last cent was gone sat on a bench opposite some vacant ground. On the lot grew some young willows. Willows suggested to him obvious thought—willow baskets. He went to a library and asked for books on basket making. After he learned how baskets were made, he returned to the willows and soon was earning a living. That was obvious thinking at every step, but it showed an original mind.

A blanket manufacturer wanted to predetermine which colors would sell best at his different prices. Instead of guessing, he went to manufacturers of rugs and bedroom furnishings. He knew that purchases of blankets were made after the rugs and curtains were bought, so it was obvious that he should select colors to harmonize with the popular hues in furnishings. This line of reasoning resulted in sure-fire lines of low-price, middle-price, and high-price blankets.

A western druggist wanted to sell umbrellas. On rainy days he put out a rack of new ones and offered to lend them, the borrower leaving a dollar deposit. But as the customer took the umbrella, the druggist said, "Of course, you don't need to return it if you don't want to." Few did. What an obvious way to sell umbrellas!

A grocer was confronted with a retailing problem common in hard times—that of the customer who says to his family, "We owe Smith so much money that I don't think we'd better go there any more." Such people often make cash purchases elsewhere. Realizing this, our grocer friend did an obvious but original thing: He wrote all his overdue customers that he would not dun them if they would give him their cash business. He expressed confidence in their willingness to pay when their affairs improved. Up went his cash sales.

Old-time packages were mere protectors and containers. Packages can do more than that, Ben Nash, a package expert, reminds us. Nash believes a package should do a real selling job, and this may be accomplished in many ways-by revealing the contents through a Cellophane window in the side of the box, by carrying a selling message on the label, through unusual shape, etc.

An ice cream manufacturer makes extra sales by filling an obvious need. He offers a brick of cream between a pint and a quart in size-specially designed for four at a bridge table.

A green insurance salesman, Vash Young, did some obvious thinking which has made him prosperous. He saw that most insurance salesmen specialized in talking the death benefits of insurance. Vash thought it obvious that more men would be interested in life benefits. So he specializes more or less in retirement annuity policies which assure an income through the later years of the wage earner and his family. That makes Vash a benefactor instead of a gloom- artist, and he sells a lot of insurance.

"Human beings have a downright horror of anything simple and direct," writes Van Dine in The Benson Murder Case.

That is why the obvious is often so original.

INSIGHTS TO IMAGINATION:

Asking yourself and others what is the most obvious need can be an eye opening exercise. How could you use B. Altman & Company's testing method for a new product or service you are to introduce?

Spend an hour one day on either your business or someone else's business. If you focus on another business, ask that business owner to focus on yours. Ask the obvious questions. Remember the question earlier in the book, "Does it have to be that way?" Apply it now for all areas of your business.

163 | watching the "stop" and "go" signs

chapter nineteen

SOMEONE HAS DISCOVERED THAT MILK KEEPS LONGER in green bottles with black stripes. The same magazine which records this fact, reports also that Professor Bergius, winner of the 1931 Nobel Prize for chemistry, has invented a process to turn wood into sugar which is cheaper and sweeter than any other sugar on the market.

Comparing these two innovations we do not have to guess long before concluding that the milk bottles win. The good professor may have a sweet which is even better for the body than sugar made from cane, corn, or beets. But "sugar made from wood!" Most people have a deep conviction that "natural" foods are best-and it seems more "natural" to make sugar from cane than from wood. So we would expect considerable resistance to wood sugar. Milk in green bottles with black stripes is a change which raises no basic doubts. Probably the most serious obstacle would be disbelief in the value claimed for the new color. People would still respect milk, and this green bottle could not possibly harm it.

"Knowledge," declared Macaulay, "advances by steps, and not by leaps." We pause before accepting that statement in all its flat finality. Nevertheless, it is true in a general way, so true that in looking at successful innovations in business we may find that Macaulay's saying can be adapted and made an excellent wall motto for our commercial laboratory—thus:

> *"Successful innovations in business are advances by steps, and not by leaps."*

WHAT WORKS AND WHAT DOESN'T

1. New business policies and new products accompanied by higher than average prices can count on success only in high-grade outlets and among consumers with high incomes.

That ought to be obvious to everyone. It is not—inventors, owners of lunch rooms, engineers, and even experienced business executives often mistakenly expect the public to pay extra for goods which may be the best of their kind but which, after all, are only slightly superior to competitive merchandise sold at substantially lower prices. The makers of a certain chocolate bar cannot understand why a rival bar made of cheaper cocoa beans outsells theirs five to one. The fact is that the poorer bar really tastes better to most consumers. This, together with its larger size, is enough to corner the business.

Rising to higher-priced merchandise, we find that radically new styles in clothing nearly always succeed first in smart specialty shops and from there work downward through less exclusive stores to end up in the bargain basements of department stores. The "tear-drop" automobile—in spite of its demonstrable superiority—starts cautiously in modified form before automobile manufacturers dare to put it into mass production. Modernistic furniture cannot go immediately to low-class furniture stores. It must first be tested in stores where customers have more imagination and are open to new ideas. And this reminds us that—

2. New steps requiring artistic or intellectual appreciation should also be launched cautiously in high-grade stores and prove acceptable to high-income groups before they can hope to win the masses.

3. *New products at low prices encounter relatively little resistance, and that resistance may vanish completely when the price gets down to a dime, a nickel, or a cent.*

Thus a new pack of cigarettes at 10 cents may by its newness and small price arouse curiosity to the buying point. A 5-cent confection, interesting and novel, may tempt many to buy just to find out what it is like. When the price drops to a penny the possible loss is so little that sales are made through mere exposure of the goods.

4. *Innovations may be risky in proportion to the general favor existing for different products or customers.*

Thus it is a question if the Franklin car with its efficient air-cooling has got as far as it might have gone had several other air-cooled automobiles been marketed successfully. The mere fact that other automobile makers cool their motors with water is enough to make some feel that air-cooling is open to question. In several cases where new products have been launched—notably the first baked beans in cans—the pioneer had slow going. Progress was faster when one or more competitors appeared to help along the new idea.

5. However—*innovations may stand out and succeed quickly for the very reason that they are so un-like competitors.* There are always people who want to be different. In one advertising campaign on which I worked, this principle was employed to save a popular product from an untimely death. True, most people like to travel with the crowd. This fact was recognized in the use of "success talk" during the building up of the product, but after a few years sales began to decline. Several surveys made it apparent that there was only one reason: many users wanted to buy something that was not quite so overwhelmingly popular. So the advertising was changed. The general popularity of this favorite was no longer referred to in the advertising. The art work was raised to a higher level. The implication in the text was that not everyone would care for a product as individual as this. Sales quickly rose again, and in a year's time had passed their previous peak.

6. A product having several parts should not introduce too many changes at one time.

This is stating in another way our belief that progress should go by steps, and not by leaps. Thus, for all I know, a new braking system might be invented which would be entirely divorced from the wheels of an automobile. But four-wheel brakes were readily accepted because they represented a simpler step forward from two-wheel brakes than some braking system which might be applied to the flywheel. Two of the old-style brakes had worked fairly well. Brakes all four wheels were easy to understand and sounded perhaps just twice as effective.

7. The merit of the new idea or product should be easily demonstrated—in advertising, and in selling either to the trade or to the final customer—whether the service or product is to be sold in a store, from door to door, by letter, or through mail-order advertising.

When he received his first cars with four-wheel brakes, a Cleveland automobile dealer found some of his prospective customers doubtful about them. He staged a demonstration at a local skating rink; here he proved dramatically that the car could stop suddenly on ice without skidding. The Fuller Brush salesman interests women because his brushes are demonstrably novel and practical. On the other hand, retail clerks kill many a promising innovation through their inability to explain or demonstrate it to the customer.

8. The innovation must appeal to the type of user for whom it is designed.

Gloucester fishermen specially pack their fish for perfect delivery to the inland customer-there is no use pushing this specialty in seacoast cities where fresh fish is available and needs no extra protection. Manufacturers of preparations to take the kink out of human hair waste no efforts on the white market—they concentrate their sales work in the African-American sections. A sharp appeal to one large group may bring more profit than a vague general appeal to the whole United States.

9. The new idea should extend the usefulness of the product, store, salesman, or division of the business.

Luminous dials make watches useful during more hours of the day. Open displays increase the usefulness of a store by quickening service. A good sample case helps the salesman to make more calls in less time.

> 1 However—many innovations merely improve the appearance of a product or store or container—and this, too, may increase sales.

> 2 The innovation should appeal to some instinct, emotion, or desire of the customer rather than offer merely an appeal to reason.

Some years ago a motor car manufacturer made his last stand by announcing a handsome automobile designed and built to give ten years of average service. I do not know how many were sold, but soon the sponsor closed his doors for good. The sales appeal had been made entirely on logic. The advertising merely described in cold, technical language the satisfaction of owning a car that would outlast all others.

Not long afterwards, the makers of Rolls-Royce came along with much the same kind of car. They reminded the public that no Rolls-Royce had ever worn out. But they went further. They did not hesitate to remind the reader that no other car cost so much. Laurence G. Meads tells me that he talked with the head salesman for Rolls-Royce in New York. That worthy had one simple sales point which worked miracles. When a lady sat down in the car, he would look at her rather reverently. Then he would say with deliberate impressiveness, "Mrs. Blitz, a woman of your social standing can't afford to be seen in any other kind of car."

Yes; an appeal to the emotions wins out every time when matched against an appeal to the head.

12. The new idea should be tested in a small way before it is put out on a large or national scale.

Parisian dressmakers show new styles to small groups of buyers before commercial production begins. No matter how foolproof a new product, policy, or business measure may seem, it should first be tried out on a small group of those to whom it must appeal to be commercially successful. One day I sat with a group of business executives discussing a plan which we all thought would appeal to people having low incomes. The head of the company had an inspiration. "Before we adopt this," he suggested, "let's call in Steve and see what he thinks of it." Steve was the janitor. Steve came in and listened patiently. Then he said, "I don't think it would work, because—" And he brought out one simple fact which the rest of us had overlooked entirely.

13. We should question the profit possibilities of anything which must show considerable loss before profits can be expected.

Unlike great originators in science or the arts, we do not, in business, work for glory or immortality. We want to make money without wasting too much time.

It is sometimes best to add a greater profit to the new product. One reason: the merchant may deserve extra earnings for his work in pushing it during the early stages. Another reason: we want to find out in the shortest possible time whether or not the new idea will work. So it may be best to launch it under slightly unfavorable conditions. The new idea should command a premium: if it cannot, its value may be questionable.

14. The new idea, to be profitable, must fit in with the prevailing mood or outlook of the public.

Men's silk shirts were best sellers in 1919 but idle shelf-warmers in 1932. Quick-cooking and ready-to-eat food specialties would probably have made little headway in the nineties. The tabloid newspaper had been tried in a more deliberate age, but it did not take. Forty years ago the advertising of Kotex and other products for feminine hygiene would have shocked women's modesty.

So business originality should always fit in with prevailing conditions and moods. It may anticipate new trends or a change that is in the making, but it must not run too far ahead: the drum major must not march a block ahead of his band. To be too much in advance of the times may be as fatal as being too far behind.

15. The innovation may be an old idea revived–such as the jig-saw puzzle and the opera hat.

In 1933, Marlene Dietrich got wide publicity by appearing at a dance in modified men's clothing. This was only a revival; as a boy I used to see Dr. Mary Walker wearing men's clothing on the streets of Oswego. Some styles are successful revivals. Even the bulging bustle enjoyed a revival some years after it was thought dead and buried. Discarded old idea in advertising and selling are sometimes revived and with little retouching go out to catch a new generation unawares.

16. The innovation may be simply some staple imported from another country.

Mah Jong. The cheeses—Limburger, Brie, Stilton, Swiss, Gorgonzola.

17. Any innovation designed to replace some other invention or different type of product may have to compromise with the old before it can hit its best stride.

The first railroad coaches looked like stagecoaches. Probably that was more sensible than making an immediate jump to some more practical form of railroad car. People should be eased into the radical change—always. Only slowly did the automobile take the form and shape best suited to it. The basic new idea in each of these examples was novel enough to stagger the imagination of early users without putting up any more hurdles than were necessary.

18. The new idea should not be discounted merely because it seems of slight importance.

To one storekeeper the idea of selling only articles priced at 5 and 10 cents might have seemed trivial; but not to Woolworth. His faith and imagination carried him right through early failures in trying to put the new idea over. Such a simple novelty as a new breadstuff—the Parker House roll—helped to make famous the Parker House in Boston. Statler captured the imagination of the traveling man by building the first moderate-rate hotel to offer a bath with every room.

19. The innovation should not be thrown away without trial merely because the same idea failed at some previous time.

About twenty years ago an automobile manufacturer failed because during one fatal year he painted all his cars with black hoods and red bodies. A few years later a new make of car offered exactly the same color combination and went over with a bang. In 1849 Mrs. Bloomer up in York State tried to popularize the garments which still bear her name. She failed, but when girls climbed astride bicycle saddles back came bloomers to make their inventor's name immortal.

20. Here is a statement which is almost a law: The probable acceptance of a new idea is in inverse proportion to its originality.

In other words, an idea that departs only 10 percent from the conventional may be acceptable to 90 percent of the population, while something which departs 90 percent from the conventional may appeal to only 10 percent of the consuming public. (Here some may remark that no originality at all is the only way to have sure-fire success with everyone—hence, this whole book has been in vain.) However, this twentieth generalization simply restates the caution previously given to move forward in easy steps. A new flaked cereal might be made of an unfamiliar African grain. At first it might meet with serious resistance. Or ready-to-eat oat flakes might be offered. Resistance to the oat flakes might be less because oats are familiar. But some women might hesitate to buy because they have been taught that oats should have long and thorough cooking. New and novel corn flakes would sell more quickly at the start because corn flakes have been popular for years.

In trying to determine which innovations have the best chance to prosper, we seem to arrive at three conclusions:

1 In business, originality should move forward by steps, not by leaps.

2 Every new style, new product, new kind of advertising, new promotion scheme should be tested in a small way before entering upon large-scale operations.

3 The fact that a little originality often goes a long way should encourage every reader of this book. Big businesses have been built from little specialties. One little idea when added to an old, conventional business often does wonders. One little change may double sales. One little idea may turn an unpromising job into a big one.

INSIGHTS TO IMAGINATION:

Review the twenty stop and go signs. The first one is critical to the success of any venture.

There are many companies that have explored and succeeded in the higher price space. They have, however, proved their benefit (real or perceived) is worth the extra investment.

Look at number six for example. Once air bags were accepted (and they started on higher end models) on the driver's side, they than went to the passenger side. Now depending on the car, SUV, or minivan, you could have upwards of eight air bags.

When anti-lock brakes were first introduced, car manufacturers showed their benefits on ice and snow. Sounds a lot like the car dealer in Cleveland Giles wrote about.

Number thirteen is probably the most important sign of the twenty. If it had been adhered to during the dot com boom and bust, just think how many billions of dollars could have been spared. The original model of that time was that we need to lose massive amounts of money in order to eventually show a profit. Giles rightly points out the fallacy of this thinking.

If we move ahead to number twenty, we see something truly astounding. Let's use electric cars and hybrid cars as our two examples of the extremes of Giles' 90/10 equation.

Electric cars gained very little acceptance when they were introduced. The notion of poor performance, the need to recharge the battery, and the inability to go long distances limited its appeal to a minute portion of the population.

Hybrids, on the other hand, offer 90% of the driving experience of a conventional car. In fact, hybrids started out at the lower end of the market and have now worked their way up to the luxury segment. Many of the hybrid applications now planned aren't necessarily to improve gas performance but rather to increase performance without reducing fuel economy.

Once again, review these twenty stop and go signs. They were true in 1934 and are just as true if not more so today.

the tragedy of a can of soup

chapter twenty

R ECENTLY, IN AN OLD FRAME HOUSE ON NOSTRAND
Avenue, Brooklyn was found what is believed to be the
oldest canned soup in existence. The label on the tin
reads, "This can of Beef Soup or Extract was put up by Daggett
& Kensett, New Haven, Conn., in the year of 1821."

James Kellogg brought the can to the Grocery Trade
News and supplied further information about it. It seems
that there were complaints in those early days about
"burned soup" and "unsatisfactory service," but the officers
of the U. S. Schooner Shark in 1824 signed a testimonial
to the effect that the products of Daggett & Kensett were
"perfectly fresh & sound, fine flavored & very agreeable to
the palate ... & being convinced of their utility we think
them particularly deserving attention, & would recom-
mend them as being very convenient & excellent provi-
sions for sea service."

During the year when this century-old can came to light,
another item about soup was printed in the newspapers. It
read: "PHILADELPHIA—Payment of the greater part of the
State inheritance tax on the estate of Dr. John T. Dorrance,
former head of the Campbell Soup Co., namely, the sum
of $14,501,330, was made to the Pennsylvania Treasury on

March 31. In addition, the executors filed a bond of $4,000,000, insuring payment of another $3,500,000."

Eighteen million dollars for one man's inheritance taxes to Pennsylvania alone—all from soup!

Daggett & Kensett were pioneers in canning soup. Why are they forgotten? Why didn't they, too, make a memorable fortune from soup? Perhaps the story of Dr. Dorrance contains a hint or two.

Dorrance studied chemistry in the Massachusetts Institute of Technology. Then he went to the University of Gottingen where he specialized in chemistry, physics, and mathematics, and won his degree as Doctor of Philosophy. In Europe he was impressed with the food value of soup and its wide popularity. He found soup served everywhere—in big cities, in small towns, in rural communities; soup kettles were present in every kitchen. Dorrance came home with the conviction that this country could be taught to appreciate soup. But American women disliked slow-cooking foods because of both cost and bother, and it took slow simmering to make soup good. Dorrance had only a little cash, but an uncle who made some two hundred food products over in Camden gave the young chemist a corner in his factory; here Dorrance began experiments with soup. The fruits of his work were destined to crowd out of the factory the other foods prepared by his uncle.

Daggett & Kensett had been pioneers in canning soup. If their failure to make millions from it may be called the tragedy of a can of soup, we may find that the reasons lie in the fact that Dorrance did not stop where they did, but went on with his creative thinking to solve all the other problems involved in popularizing soup.

He saw that the bulky non-condensed canned soups which existed at that time cost too much to handle and ship.

He realized that the highest possible quality was of vital importance if soup were to be made popular in every home.

He knew that people must be taught the definite food value of soup.

To solve these problems, he began by condensing Campbell's Soup so that a given quantity would go twice as far as other soups.

He improved the quality again and again through study of soups both here and abroad.

He advertised. He had to use small space at the start, for the company had little money; but as time went on, Campbell's Soups had back of them one of the biggest advertising appropriations in the country. Several prominent advertising men even thought that Campbell's was advertised too heavily—but never Dr. Dorrance.

Thus he proved that creative thinking, taking one step after another, could build a huge fortune without much initial capital. His story is similar to that of many other successful men—perseverance and follow-through are quite as important as getting new ideas.

In an article in the *Cosmopolitan Magazine*, Samuel Crowther reminds us: "John D. Rockefeller did not discover petroleum; he entered a zone which was already so crowded as to be unstable. James B. Duke bucked one of the oldest lines in the South when he began trading in tobacco, while, when A. T. Stewart wanted to open a store in New York, the retail merchandising field was so crowded that no one would grant him credit. He was forced to buy slightly used sample goods at auction for cash. These he made to look like new and sold them for low prices."

CHANGE IS CONSTANT

Bruce Barton unearthed this choice remark made by Samuel Johnson in 1759: "The trade of advertising is now so near to perfection that it is not easy to propose any improvement."

If my memory serves rightly, it was less than a hundred years later that a man named Hone threw up his job in the United States Patent Office because he thought that mechanical invention had reached such a state of perfection that there was no future in it.

Today, few believe that perfection has been reached in any direction. We know that the horizon expands as we advance, and that every scientific discovery, mechanical invention, or business method opens a gate to other pastures. We realize the necessity of cultivating new ideas if we are to make any kind of living and derive any real satisfaction from our work.

One of the surest ways to get new ideas is to expect them with confidence. But how can we increase our expectancy? What gives us the right to believe that we, too, can be original thinkers?

WHERE IS YOUR BEST CHANCE?

At the risk of repetition, let us look at some questions which we should ask in attempting to find just where and just how we can go farthest with our imagination. We have looked at the processes and successes of other innovators. We have examined the characteristics of people so that we might know how to fit our ideas with their wants and creatable desires. A few chapters back I quoted a welfare worker and some of her key questions used to wake people up to what they could do best. Here are other questions suggested for self-examination. They may throw light on the kind of work which offers each of us our best chance of being original.

"What business activity arouses my greatest enthusiasm?" Perhaps four out of five are square pegs in round holes and can have no great enthusiasm in their work, but as Emerson says, "Nothing great was ever achieved without enthusiasm." Familiarity with the lives of men and women confirms Emerson's statement. In the long run the best ideas come only in that activity which arouses our greatest enthusiasm, provided always that we do not become mere fanatics about some fantastic theory. This will also be the work which is so refreshing that we can work harder at it and for longer periods of time without fatigue. In a sense, Dorrance consecrated his life to soup and that explains his success. He said that the only three things in his life were his wife, his children, and soup. If you are enthusiastic about accounting, you will probably do better at that

in the long run than you will by trying to become a salesman merely because salesmanship seems more lucrative. Ideas come most abundantly to us in those fields which hold our greatest interest, and one sure test of fitness for a position is the degree of enthusiasm we can bring to it.

"In what direction have I the most experience and confidence?" Experience leads to confidence and so opens the way to new ideas. There are mystic aspects to the process of getting new ideas, but plain common sense tells us that the more we know about a subject the richer our ideas will be about it. This is apparently contradicted by the fact that many innovations in business come from outsiders, people who are inexperienced amateurs. But their interest and enthusiasm supply inspiration which makes up for their apparent lack of specialized knowledge. Specialized knowledge coupled with the same interest and enthusiasm usually goes further. Where people fail in spite of their expertness, it is usually due to their belief that they, like Hone, have nothing more to learn—that the uttermost boundaries have been reached, and that no continents are left unexplored.

"If all vocations paid equal rewards and involved equal labor, which would I choose?" This is related to the previous questions but it serves to bring home more sharply the need to know just what we want most to do. A professor in one of the eastern colleges advises students to select their vocations without regard to economic considerations. One student disregarded this advice and for some years he tried to make a living as a woolen salesman. He was discontented and below par in health. One day the professor's counsel came back to him and he mentioned it to his wife. "Well," asked she, "what would you like to do most?" He felt almost ashamed of his answer—but he thought that nothing would make him happier than making reproductions of choice pieces of Colonial furniture. Today that is his *occupation and he is earning far more money than he ever did at salesmanship.*

We look too much at the dollar under our nose and miss the pot of gold at the end of the one road in the world which, of all men, we can travel best. To paraphrase Shakespeare: "And this above all; to thine own self be true and it must follow as the night the day thou canst not fail to achieve some degree of originality" and "The labor we delight in physics pain and stimulates inventiveness."

"TOO MANY IRONS—"

Take with a grain of salt the old advice against having too many irons in the fire. Some business men admit freely that their reputations as originators have grown from the fact that their few successes are remembered while their many failures are forgotten. They had to sow many new ideas to bring comparatively few through to harvest. It is the same with inventors, artists, writers, architects. No doubt a fascinating story could be written about Edison's failures. Once he wanted to put a huge phonograph in the Statue of Liberty to warn mariners of approaching storms. At another time he thought that Congress would appreciate a mechanical device to record their votes instantly. By pressing buttons all Congressmen could vote simultaneously on a measure. But, no; that idea was thrown promptly out the window, for Congress wanted parliamentary formality and the sound of their resonant "ayes" and "nays." After that experience Edison made a sage remark. "Never again will I invent something which people do not want."

Cartwright is remembered for his invention of the power loom. But Cartwright planned fireproofing houses, invented machinery to bake bread and biscuits, invented bricks on a geometrical system, worked out a new three-furrow plow, won medals for essays on manure and potato growing, helped Fulton with his steamship, was awarded patents for making ropes, calendering linen, and cutting velvet pile.

Watt is remembered for his steam engine but he, too, had many irons in the fire—most of which are forgotten. He invented a letter copying machine, another machine for producing illuminating gas from coal, a new kind of clock, a micrometer, a novel oil lamp, and a machine for reproducing sculpture.

SILK PURSES FROM SOWS' EARS

Edward Battey tells me that recently there was displayed in Paris a silk purse made from a sow's ear. Well, after seeing silk stockings made from wood, why not? Thus is the wisdom of ancient proverbs upset. Did Daggett & Kensett realize how profitable they might have made canned soup? Perhaps not. Sometimes we do not trust our new ideas enough—or is it that we mistrust our ability to do something with them?

Back in 1857, Sir William J. Herschel wrote to his brother Alexander: "I want a writing machine— a piano that shall print a letter for each note I touch. What's the difficulty?

"I want a box with little knobs on the surface arranged so as to fit the fingers as the hand is put down on the table— one set for the right hand and one for the left, the paper to lie in the middle on a traversing platform. And as each note is pressed I want the hammers of the piano to come down and stamp their letters on the paper, shifting the paper at the same time, of course."

But Herschel was unfaithful to his vision of the writing machine and perhaps it wandered through the ether to America where it was met with a warmer welcome.

Shorthand methods had been used for centuries before Sir Isaac Pitman perfected a system worthy of general and widespread acceptance. The ancients had steam turbines of a sort, but thousands of years passed before some one made them practical for industry. Over twenty years ago I helped sell a motor truck which had non-clashing gears. It is only yesterday that this mechanical advantage was built into passenger cars.

Getting new ideas is not enough. We must give them the same chance in life that we want to give our children. We must nurse them to maturity, push them into the stream of life, and be ready to rush to the rescue if danger threatens. Let's not have our canned soup found in a musty attic a hundred years hence!

I venture to close with this from Goethe:

Are you in earnest? Seize this very minute; What you can do, or dream you can, begin it; Boldness has genius, power and magic in it; Only engage and then the mind grows heated; Begin, and then the work will be completed.

INSIGHTS TO IMAGINATION:

Who would you rather be, Daggett and Kensett or Dr. James T. Dorrance?

Dr. Dorrance. Review the list of problems Dr. Dorrance solved in order to make Campbell's Soup.

While it's exciting and potentially lucrative to be a pioneer Giles is suggesting there is more money to be made and good to be done by improving a good or service that already exists.

To wrap up this chapter, Giles presents us with some thought provoking questions. I've included them here again because your answers will be enlightening.

What business activity arouses my greatest enthusiasm?

In what direction do I have the most experience and confidence?

If all vocations paid equal rewards and involved equal labor, which would I choose?

RON KLEIN 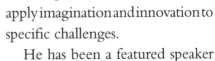 is a teacher of creativity and innovation. He offers keynote addresses that inspire imagination and innovation. He conducts seminars that develop creativity in individuals. Ron consults with companies and organizations to

apply imagination and innovation to specific challenges.

He has been a featured speaker at the Napoleon Hill World Learning Center. He has also been profiled in Bottom Line Personal.

Ron is currently working on bringing a series of long-lost books on creativity and innovation back to today's audience.

RAY GILES, the author of "Turn Your Imagination Into Money!," was a partner in the Blackman-Ross Company, one of New York's leading advertising agencies in the early part of the 20th century.

During his twenty years of agency experience he has worked with many of America's largest manufacturers in formulating advertising and other sales promotion measures for their products.

Hundreds of articles by Mr. Giles have appeared in the Saturday Evening Post, Colliers', Literary Digest,

 Advertising & Selling, Printers' Ink, Reader's Digest and in other publications both here and abroad. He was author of twelve books—including "500 Answers to Sales Objections" (Ronald Press), "Breaking Through Competition" (Appleton) and "Developing and Managing Salesmen" (Ronald Press).

THANK YOU for purchasing *Turn Your Imagination Into Money*. Please visit www.morgan-james.com/imagination to collect your free bonus.

Please go to the website below to share your story, or someone's story you know of, on how you turned your imagination into money. We will be coming out with a series of success stories and would love to include yours.

www.turnyourimaginationintomoney.com

9 781933 596587